MOBILE AND WIRELESS NETWORKS SECURITY

T0321621

MOBILE AND WIRELESS NETWORKS SECURITY

Proceedings of the MWNS 2008 Workshop
Singapore   9 April 2008

editors

Maryline Laurent-Maknavicius
Hakima Chaouchi

TELECOM SudParis, France

 **World Scientific**

NEW JERSEY · LONDON · SINGAPORE · BEIJING · SHANGHAI · HONG KONG · TAIPEI · CHENNAI

Published by

World Scientific Publishing Co. Pte. Ltd.

5 Toh Tuck Link, Singapore 596224

USA office: 27 Warren Street, Suite 401-402, Hackensack, NJ 07601

UK office: 57 Shelton Street, Covent Garden, London WC2H 9HE

British Library Cataloguing-in-Publication Data
A catalogue record for this book is available from the British Library.

MOBILE AND WIRELESS NETWORKS SECURITY
Proceedings of the MWNS 2008 Workshop

ISBN-13 978-981-283-325-9 (pbk)
ISBN-10 981-283-325-0 (pbk)

Printed in Singapore.

CONTENTS

MESSAGE FROM THE GENERAL CHAIRS

Information and Communication technology is nowadays undeniably the fundamental pillar of any company seeking a high level of effectiveness, and reactivity. In fact, communication technologies made it possible to improve productivity, and have constrained the companies to adapt their working methods to survive to market competition. However, one cannot ignore the existence of intrinsic and extrinsic vulnerabilities of these communication systems, which confers on networks security fundamental role. Even if networks have evolved from wired to wireless networks, network security objectives remained the same for both; to preserve integrity, confidentiality and availability of information and networks resources. Several mechanisms have been developed to achieve these goals. For instance, we can mention authentication, encryption, access control... According to the network environment, certain security mechanisms are not mature enough due to the youth of certain network technologies such as wireless, ad hoc or sensor networks. However, even with the maturity, and even if they are already largely implemented in the market network security products, like firewalls and VPNs, certain mechanisms still need improvements. It is also important to consider resource limitations of mobile terminals and radio-communications in order to adapt security mechanisms of wired networks to wireless networks' context. We attend a major evolution of networks that could be summarized by the need to allow the user to communicate in any place statically or while moving. This was possible thanks to the evolution of wireless and mobile networks, and the evolution of mobile terminals' design. Even if security solutions are not yet finalized in those environments, the deployment of wireless networks is already effective and will tend to be deployed even more because of the increasing need of user's mobility, flexibility and services. In order to achieve this challenge, industrial and academic research groups are working on one hand developing wireless and mobile technologies, with or without infrastructure, offering more and more resources and security, and on the other hand, developing autonomous terminals increasingly powerful (PDA, telephones...). This workshop (MWNS 2008) is a first initiative to gather security researchers in both wireless and mobile networks so that they can present their latest research results in this field and provide good discussion about the existing security issues and challenges in this resource limited and easy spying networks; the wireless and mobile networks.

Hakima Chaouchi, Maryline Laurent-Maknavicius
Editors of a French book by Hermes 2007 "Security of wireless and mobile networks", 3 volumes.

MWNS 2008 COMMITTEES

Workshop Chairs

M. Maknavicius   Institut TELECOM, TELECOM &
H. Chaouchi   Management SudParis, France

Technical Program Chair

O. Heen Thomson R&D, France   Thomson R&D, France

Technical Program Committee

K. Al Agha   LRI, France
N. Alonistioti   University of Pireus, Greece
J. Araujo   Alcatel-Lucent, France
J.W. Atwood   Concordia University, Canada
F. Bader   CTTC, Spain
A.-L. Beylot   ENSEEIHT, France
A. Bouabdallah   UTC, France
H. Chaouchi   TELECOM & Management SudParis
I. Chrisment   Nancy University, France
V. Friderikos   Centre for Telecommunication Research
                          of London, UK
I. Ganchev   University of Limerick, Ireland
M. Gerlach   Fokus, Germany
W. Haddad   Ericsson, Sweden
A. Hecker   TELECOM ParisTech, France
O. Heen   Thomson R&D, France
J. Leneutre   TELECOM ParisTech, France
M. Maknavicius   Telecom & Management SudParis, France
K. Masmoudi   Cyber Networks, France

A. Mellouk	University Paris 12, France
M. Minier	INSA-Lyon, France
H. Moustafa	France Telecom, France
P. Muhlethaler	INRIA, France
J.M. Nogueira	UFMG, Brazil
M. O'Droma,	University of Limerick, Ireland
O. Rojas	Instituto Tecnologico de Jiquilpan, Mexico
P. Schoo	DoCoMo Euro-Labs, Germany
A. Serhrouchni	TELECOM ParisTech, France

TOWARD A NEW AD HOC NODE DESIGN FOR SECURE SERVICE DEPLOYMENT OVER AD HOC NETWORK[*]

HAKIMA CHAOUCHI

Institut TELECOM, TELECOM & Management SudParis, France
LOR/SAMOVAR/CNRS UMR-5157

MARYLINE LAURENT-MAKNAVICIUS

Institut TELECOM, TELECOM & Management SudParis, France
LOR/SAMOVAR/CNRS UMR-5157

Abstract- Security in ad hoc networks is a major issue when it comes to real deployment of services over this sort of networks. A large amount of research effort was directed toward routing in ad hoc networks, however securing the connectivity and the packet transmission is a brake in relying on an ad hoc network as any other infrastructure based network. In this paper, we propose a secured architecture over ad hoc network based on the AAA concept (Authentication, Authorisation, Accounting), and a new ad hoc nodes design for any kind of ad hoc nodes to securely support part or full AAA services.

1. Introduction

Ad hoc network is dynamically changing its network topology. It is an infrastructure-less network created by mobile nodes in an ad hoc way. In an ad hoc network, mobile nodes come and go as they wish, so the topology of the network is changing quite rapidly. This creates new challenges for the routing protocols to be used in ad hoc networks. Most of the traditional protocols don't fit very well into ad hoc networks. New routing protocols [1, 2] were developed but none of them is really deployed.

In the context of Always On era, ad hoc technologies integration with the infrastructure is without any doubt an interesting approach for extending at low cost the network access coverage. However a real and business oriented service deployment over ad hoc network requires firstly security of the communications and resource accounting. The lack of security and accounting mechanisms is the major issue that slows down the deployment of ubiquitous services. We believe

---

[*] This work was performed in the context of the French research project SARAH, ANR 2006

that the integration of ad hoc and infrastructure-based technologies coupled with efficient security and accounting techniques is the answer for the urgent demand of network operators for appropriate architectures to host secure and large scale ubiquitous services.

There are several threats in ad hoc networks. First, those related to wireless data transmission such as eavesdropping, message replaying, message distortion and active impersonation. Second, those related to ad hoc construction of the network. This means that attacks can come also from inside the ad hoc network. Therefore we cannot trust one centralized node, because if this node would be compromised the whole network would be useless. Another problem is scalability. Ad hoc networks can have hundreds or even thousands of mobile nodes. This introduces important challenges to security mechanisms [3].

As most of the security issues in ad hoc networks are caused by trustless nodes, the authentication process is a strong solution to identify misbehaving nodes. Nevertheless, ensuring authentication service in a self organized network is not easy to realize. We propose in this work to build a secured ad hoc infrastructure framework where the AAA service which is classically centralized in the infrastructure network is decomposed into three sub-services and partly executed by the infrastructure network. The authentication service (Aaa), the authorization and accounting services (aAA). These services will be securely distributed by the servicing ad hoc nodes. For this purpose, a trust management framework is necessary. Furthermore, we propose a new design of ad hoc nodes that enables any kinds of ad hoc nodes to securely support part or full AAA services, and to act as individual or delegated ad hoc service providers to other ad hoc nodes.

One obvious and original consequence of the secured framework and node design would be the integration of ad hoc technology in the service value chain by the introduction of a new service provider (ad hoc network service provider), and a new network access provider (ad hoc network). Users provided with one or more suitably designed ad hoc node(s) are also able to join the service value chain by offering their nodes capacity to some well known ad hoc (service or network access) providers. The classical operator then will make profit by offering in addition to his classical services (access to Internet), new services for ad hoc nodes. For instance, it will act as a third party between the servicing ad hoc nodes, and the customers (local ad hoc nodes). The operator acting as a third party for the servicing and served ad hoc nodes will guarantee the AAA service and a secured transaction for exchanged services (peer-to-peer, packet forwarding, resource consumption…).

2. AAA in ad hoc networks

Typically authentication, authorization, and accounting are more or less dependent on each other. However, separate protocols are used to achieve the AAA functionality. IETF AAA working group is trying to design one AAA protocol that could be used in a variety of applications. The IRTF AAAARCH group is also trying to build a general architecture for AAA systems. Mobile Ad Hoc networking (MANET) brings new challenges to providing the AAA functionality. Ad Hoc networks are by their nature rapidly changing and dynamic. There isn't necessarily any network infrastructure present. These and other features of ad hoc networks present many new requirements for security protocols in ad hoc networks [4].

Several research works are conducted on the classically centralized AAA functions [5, 6], but very few studied the possible interactions between AAA and ad hoc network. For instance, [7] focuses mainly on the authentication architecture for enabling distant users to access to services (like internet) through an ad hoc network.

Authentication is necessary in ad hoc network as in wired network to help identify the participating nodes to the ad hoc network. Of course, authentication is not enough to secure communications between ad hoc nodes. One way to deal with low physical security and availability constraints is the distribution of trust [4]. Trust can be distributed to a collection of nodes. If all t+1 nodes will be unlikely compromised, then a consensus of t+1 nodes is trustworthy [3].

Authorization is also needed to avoid malicious host to be able to wreak havoc inside the network. This can be prevented by keeping control of what hosts are allowed to do inside the ad hoc network. Authorization also needs some sort of distributed structure to avoid single point of failure. This is why the traditional way of using *access control lists* (ACL) in one central server isn't adequate in ad hoc networks.

Accounting features are quite specialized in ad hoc networks. Because basically there is no network infrastructure that is providing the service, there isn't either the same kind of service provider concept as in traditional networks. In ad hoc networks, individual mobile hosts are providing service to each others. There can be two cases in the charging point of view. One is the case where there is no need to use charging. In this situation all the hosts have decided together that they want to form an ad hoc network for their own need to communicate with each other free of charge. This could mean that they all belong to the same organization like in the case of military units or they are in the same place and want to communicate like in a meeting. So, this sort of ad hoc network is like an intranet. In the other case, individual mobile nodes are just participating in the network to communicate with other nodes. In this case, if some mobile node acts as a router in the network, providing connectivity between two nodes that are not within each others range, then it would be reasonable to charge some money for this service [4].

It is true that ad hoc networks started within common interest communities, where charging was probably not the first goal. With the generalisation of small communicating devices other situations will arise where collaboration is technically possible, but where participants will demand a fair reward for it. Thus, the need for precise ad hoc accounting is likely to increase in next decade.

2.1. AAA systems

Ad hoc networks and general AAA systems can be seen as oxymoron. The biggest problem is related to the varying nature of the network. There are no home domains or foreign domains, because the networks are built in an ad hoc way. Also the term service provider will have different meaning than before. This affects the existing AAA systems because some of the basic building blocks of their architecture are missing from the ad hoc networks. In fact the existing AAA architecture is centralized whereas ad hoc network is decentralized.

One approach [4] to provide authentication and authorization functionalities in ad hoc networks could be to use trust management based approaches like PolicyMaker or Keynote2. These are decentralized by nature and can provide the requested functionality in ad hoc networks quite easily. Also other protocols like SASL or ISAKMP/IKE could be used to provide the authentication functionality.

3. Related work: AAA architecture over infrastructure based ad hoc networks

As described in [8], the introduction of AAA into ad hoc environment is not an easy task due to the self organising aspect of the ad hoc network. The objective of this approach is to design a functional bridge (architecture) between the ad hoc network and the infrastructure network when it is available to support secured exchange of services between the ad hoc nodes. The designed architecture named AdIN (Ad hoc/Infrastructure) is represented in Figure 1. It targets deploying several mechanisms such as authentication, authorization, accounting, and key management. Neighbour and Service discovery mechanisms are also necessary to provide information for the ad hoc node in order to allow him get the appropriate service.

The main features of AdIN architecture are [8]:
- available service within ad hoc nodes;
- neighbour and service discovery;
- user identification and anonymity. Note that user anonymity is bringing new challenges with AAA in particular with charging.
- AAA as a basis for securing communications between ad hoc nodes;
- trust management within ad hoc nodes. Note, that in an infrastructure connection, the connected node is trusted based on his successful authentication. Since the node is connected all the time, his re-authentication, which is necessary to maintain the trust relationship with the network, is transparent to the node. In the case of ad hoc connection, since the connectivity is opportunistic to the infrastructure, the re-authentication within the ad hoc network should rely on the ad hoc nodes acting as authenticators during the time where the infrastructure is unreachable.

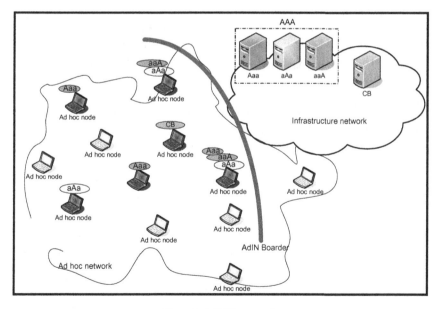

Figure 1. AdIN Framework

AdIN framework suggests decomposing the AAA service in the infrastructure into Aaa, aAa, and aaA services in order to offer them completely or separately to the ad hoc network. Another strong point of this architecture is the delegation of one or all of these services (Aaa, aAa, aaA) into certain nodes of the ad hoc network. These nodes are supposed to be secure and trusted by the infrastructure. There might be nodes that belong to the infrastructure network administration (i.e. airport buses equipped with ad hoc material). These nodes might be freely moving in the ad hoc network carrying with them the AAA services. The carried AAA services would be offered to the ad hoc network, when this one could not join the infrastructure network and benefit from the AAA service located in the infrastructure. This delegation of AAA services to the ad hoc network assumes a trusted relationship between those ad hoc nodes capable of offering the AAA services.

The aAA services could be implemented by the ad hoc nodes that are willing to provide services to the other nodes (content delivery or exchange, packets forwarding, Internet access ...). So these services (aAa, aaA) might be easily distributed in the ad hoc network as long as an accounting and billing system is in place.

The Aaa service is more difficult to distribute totally since it authenticates users joining the ad hoc network. Those users are not known by the ad hoc network. That is why it is necessary to ensure an interdomain authentication between the ad hoc network and the infrastructure network. This interdomain signalling will be ensured by the AdIN boarder represented in figure 1.

Finally the Charging and Billing (CB) service as represented in the figure could be offered by the infrastructure to the ad hoc nodes. It means that the infrastructure will be aware of the services exchanges between the ad hoc nodes and will charge the serviced ad hoc nodes for that. The servicing ad hoc node will get the payment for the service offered and will also pay the infrastructure network for supporting the CB on his behalf. As for the authentication (Aaa), authorisation (aAa) and accounting (aaA) services the infrastructure network will make profit on the usually not directly billed service which is here the CB.

In [8], we considered those AAA services to be hosted by some ad hoc nodes belonging to some administrative providers. In the next section, thanks to the proposed design of ad hoc nodes, those AAA ad hoc nodes can also be owned by users.

4. A proposed AAA architecture over infrastrureless/standalone ad hoc network

We consider a scenario depicted on figure 2 where we can build in a secured and ad hoc way a connected network based on special ad hoc nodes belonging either to providers or individuals. We introduce new ad hoc nodes pre-configured by a network or service provider to allow the establishment of an ad hoc network that will be used either to offer application services (video, network games, ...), ad hoc connectivity or internet connectivity. [9] presents an approach for pre-configuring ad hoc nodes. Those nodes might be certified as supporting ad hoc services, and sold to users as generating possible profits. In the case of internet connectivity, it will be an infrastructure based ad hoc network [8]. There will be an issue in the case where several providers will compete to gain more service opportunities. This will be a good opportunity to make an effort for standardization and interoperability, otherwise there will be proprietary AAA services not shared between providers. This last case is not optimal but still much better than the current situation where ad hoc networks are not used for service deployment. We consider the usage of the ad hoc network for service deployment within the ad hoc nodes. It means that some ad hoc nodes will host servers. The other ad hoc nodes will connect to these ad hoc servers to get services.

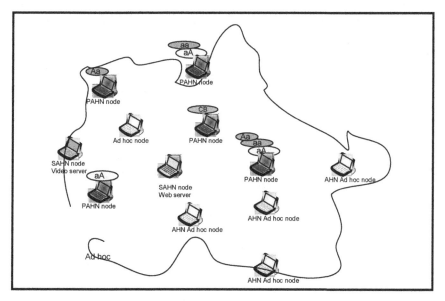

Figure 2. Ad hoc network based on Preconfigured ad hoc nodes

We name:
- PAHN (Preconfigured Ad Hoc Node); the ad hoc nodes pre-configured by a network provider to launch a secure ad hoc network offering ad hoc connectivity. It is offering mainly AAA services.
- SAHN (Servicing Ad Hoc Node); the ad hoc node hosting an application based server (web content, video…). It can be preconfigured by a service provider extending their service to an ad hoc area.
- GAHN (Gateway Ad Hoc node); the ad hoc node offering access to internet. It is similar to a PAHN in the architecture; it is different in the offered service which is here the connectivity to internet.
- AHN an Ad Hoc Node.

These nodes will be designed with separated parts, thanks to the virtualisation concept where each of them is running separately from the others a specific environment at a same time. In these new designed ad hoc nodes, one part will run the user environment, another part will run the secured connectivity related part (PAHN) and another one can run a service (SAHN) related part. This is illustrated on the figures below. It is also possible to consider a separation on network side or on a physical side. In the first case, one single network interface will be used for both user traffic and ad hoc network related traffic (using ad hoc routing). In the second case, two separate network interfaces will be used where one is dedicated for the user's traffic and the other one is used for the ad hoc network traffic. In this case we'll make sure that the user has no access at all to the traffic forwarded by his ad hoc node. In both cases the users agreed with the service or network provider to use their node as an ad hoc node which means that it will forwards other node's traffic. This agreement is defined in specific terms of the business model including the ad hoc nodes in the value chain [8].

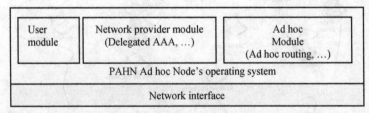

Figure 3. Pre-configured ad hoc node (PAHN) with a unique network card.(Virtualisation at network layer)

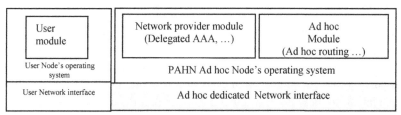

Figure 4. Pre-configured ad hoc node (PAHN) with two network cards; one for user traffic and the other is dedicated for the traffic of the other ad hoc nodes (Virtualisation at all layers, physical separation between user environment and the ad hoc treatment environment).

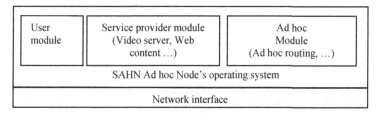

Figure 5. Pre-configured ad hoc node (SAHN) with a unique network card.(Virtualisation at network layer)

It is also possible for the ad hoc node to be PAHN and SAHN at a same time. In that case, both service provider and network provider modules will be located in the ad hoc node.

Note that a smartcard technology can be used to securely implement the network provider or server provider related environment. We can also use the virtualization technology to maintain the separation between the different modules.

The main application of these new designed ad hoc nodes is a fast deployment of a connected network without a real time support of the AAA service of the infrastructure, and with no mandatory presence of administrative ad hoc nodes. In fact the AAA service is preconfigured on the PAHN, thus allowing the authentication of the ad hoc nodes forming the network. This ad hoc network is created to provide networked applications and not internet access. In the case where internet access is needed, the GAHN are needed as well in the ad hoc node to provide a gateway service from the ad hoc node to the internet infrastructure.

5. Conclusion

The infrastructure network (network and service providers) will benefit from integrating the ad hoc technology in the access network since it will bring more users in the network. In this paper, we introduce a pre-configured ad hoc nodes design in order to build a secure ad hoc network that will support service deployment. In these pre-configured ad hoc nodes, the usually centralized AAA service will be offered by those ad hoc nodes in the ad hoc network (hybrid or standalone). Other services such as application based will be offered by other preconfigured ad hoc nodes. This will expand the service deployment of service providers to a standalone ad hoc network. The major issue will remain in battery consumption of those ad hoc nodes.

References

1. M. Guerrero Zapata. Secure Ad hoc On-Demand Distance Vector Routing. ACM Mobile Computing and Communications Review (MC2R), vol. 6, no. 3, pp. 106–107, July 2002.
2. Y. C. Hu, A. Perrig and D. B. Johnson. Ariadne: A secure on-demand routing protocol for Ad Hoc networks. In proceedings of the 8th ACM International Conference on Mobile Computing and Networking, 2002.
3. L. Zhou and Z. J. Haas. Securing Ad Hoc Networks. IEEE Network Magazine, vol. 13, no.6, November/December 1999.
4. S. Levijoki. Authentication, Authorization and Accounting in Ad Hoc networks. 2000, http://www.tml.tkk.fi/Opinnot/Tik-110.551/2000/papers/authentication/aaa.htm
5. R. Marin Lopez, J. Bournelle, J.-M. Combes, M. Laurent-Maknavicius and A.F. Gomez Skarmeta. Improved EAP keying framework for a secure mobility access service. International Wireless Communications and Mobile Computing Conference IWCMC 2006, Published in ACM Digital Library, Conference, Vancouver, Canada, July 2006.
6. J. Bournelle, M. Laurent-Maknavicius, G. Giaretta, I. Guardini, E. Demaria and L. Marchetti. Bootstrapping Mobile IPv6 using EAP. Joint IEEE Malaysia International Conference on Communications and IEEE International Conference on Networks, MICC-ICON 2005, Lumpur, Malaysia, November 2004.
7. O. Cheikhrouhou, M. Laurent-Maknavicius and H. Chaouchi. Security architecture in a multi-hop mesh network., 5ème conférence sur la Sécurité et Architectures Réseaux SAR 2006, Seignosse, Landes, France, juin 2006.
8. H. Chaouchi and M. Maknavicius. SAACCESS: Secured Ad hoc ACCess framework. International Conference on New Technologies, Mobility and

Security NTMS'07, ISBN 978-1-4020-6269-8, Paris, pp. 421-434, April-May 2007.

9. N. Pringent, C. Bidan, J.-P. Andreaux and O. Heen. Secure long term Communities in AD hoc Networks. In SASN'03: Proceedings of the 1st ACM workshop on Security of ad hoc and sensor networks, pages 115-124, New York, NY, USA, 2003. ACM.

TCA: TOPOLOGY CHANGE ATTACK IN PEER-TO-PEER NETWORKS

MAHDI ABDELOUAHAB, HANI RAGAB HASSEN, AND ABDELMADJID
BOUABDALLAH

*HeuDiaSyC, UMR CNRS 6599 University of Technology of Compiegne (UTC)
PB 20529, 60205 Compiègne, France*

MOHAMMED ACHEMLAL, AND SYLVIE LANIEPCE

*France Telecom R&D
42 rue des Coutures PB 6243, CAEN, France*

Peer-to-peer systems are overlay applications in which every computer or node has a client and server role. Some of these systems use servers to locate resources over the network but not to transfer data. Efficient operator services (ADSL) and the drop in hardware cost have led to extensive Internet spread to public consumers. Nowadays, file sharing is the most popular and used P2P application over Internet. Because of this, P2P systems are receiving considerable research attention. It is crucial to identify and characterise both vulnerabilities and attacks related to this application, in order to prevent their negative impacts. In this paper, we present a new attack: The Topology Change (TCA) attack over the eDonkey network. Further, we investigate and study scenarios and techniques used to accomplish TC Attack. Efficient deployment of such an attack may have a dangerous impact on the overlay network, especially regarding the underlying network infrastructure.

1. Introduction

A Peer-to-Peer (P2P) network is composed of a distributed architecture, theoretically with no hierarchical organization, though this is not always true in practice. P2P is designed to facilitate resource sharing (content, storage, CPU cycles) between a large number of computers, bypassing a centralized authority such as a centralized server. It is used in many different areas: grid computing, IP telephony, and instant messaging. However, the most popular P2P application is file sharing, which allows users to exchange files easily: eDonkey [6,4] and BitTorren [16] are common examples.

Peer-to-Peer allows nodes to be clients or servers. When a node A requests a specific resource from another node B, A is considered as a client and B as a server.

P2P systems are classified according to two criteria: structure and centralization [1]. A P2P system is called "unstructured", when the location of the resource is completely independent from overlay topology. In opposition, "structured" P2P systems depend on the network topology, and files are stored at specified locations (Chord [13], Tapestry [15], Pastry [14]). Structured systems provide mapping between content (e.g. file identifier) and location (e.g. node address). Centralization refers to whether all the nodes have the same hierarchical level or not, and is classified as follows:

1. Fully decentralized architectures: all nodes perform exactly the same tasks and there is no central coordination of their activities.
2. Partially centralized architectures: the basis is the same as for the fully distributed architecture; however, some nodes may locally index peer resources.
3. Hybrid decentralized architecture: in this category, an indexing server is used. This server facilitates the search operation. Data exchange can be done via a direct connection between peers and not through the server.

eDonkey is one of the most popular and widely-used P2P systems. It is an unstructured P2P system using servers to index shared files. To join the eDonkey network, a client node has to (1) register with a known eDonkey server, (2) record its information on the server: IP address and port number, (3) publish its shared files: name, size, extension, etc. Once this connection is established, the client node is ready to download files: (1) it sends a query to the server using keywords; (2) the server replies with a list of shared files that may interest the client; (3) by choosing a file F from this list, the client sends a new query to the server; (4) the server replies with a list of nodes (IP addresses) from which the client may download the desired file; (5) finally, the client downloads the file from several sources simultaneously.

Each client in the eDonkey network maintains a list of servers in the "server.dat" file, which can be obtained in different ways: (1) From the eMule's source code (pre-configured), (2) From known web sites, (3) From eDonkey servers (4) From eDonkey clients.

Jia Yang et al. [11] listed all known eDonkey servers and showed the countries sheltering these servers. The number was 253 for Germany and 248 for USA. They drew up a top-ten table listing the eDonkey servers that have the largest numbers of connected clients. The average number of connected clients per server is over 500,000. According to [10], eDonkey traffic occupies more than 40% of the whole traffic on Internet. Therefore, eDonkey security should be studied. Other issues also raise the alarm about eDonkey security; we can cite the following: all clients use the same software – eMule, so they are all vulnerable to the same attack and eDonkey connections remain open for long periods. This is not the case for traditional Internet services: web and mail. Users download very large files (audio/ video), which takes a long time. So machines are kept connected for days.

In this paper, we present possible attacks related to P2P applications. These attacks exist in classic Internet architecture (client/server) but their impact can be especially dangerous in P2P because of P2P characteristics. Indeed, since P2P is an overlay application, some attacks do not only affect the functionality of the application, but they also affect the underlying network infrastructure, generating congestion, faulty routing, etc. Our studies have led us to focus on attacks that have a considerable impact on the underlying networks (ISPs). We describe here a new attack which can harm an ISP infrastructure. Topology change attacks, when well conducted, allow an attacker to disrupt internet operating and can lead to Denial of Service at the level of ISP equipment (routers, switches).

The rest of this paper is organized as follows: Section 2 lists P2P attacks and their impact. In section 3, we (1) define the topology change attack in the case of eDonkey; (2) describe all attack scenarios and how an attacker can launch these. In section 4, we synthesise all these scenarios in four attack cases, showing their true impact. Finally, section 5 concludes this paper with a summary of major research contributions and outlines future work.

2. P2P Attacks

We present P2P attacks in this section. Most of these attacks are well known in client/server environments. We predict a dramatic impact on P2P clients if these attacks were deployed over a P2P network. The number of machines affected would be higher compared to that in a client/server environment. In practice, one real attack may consist of a single attack, as described below, or a combination of several P2P attacks. The large number of connected clients and the P2P overlay application nature offer a propitious environment for attackers.

2.1. *P2P Worms*

Worms are automated programs that exploit vulnerabilities in computers. Once they have successfully infected a system, they continue to search for new victims and can spread through the network automatically [12,2]. Usually, worms spend a considerable time during their propagation to generate random IP addresses. Each generated address represents a potential victim to which the worm can propagate. In P2P, worms detect new victims by following the overlay topology. Thus, P2P worms can propagate faster than in client/server architecture. Other reasons supporting our judgement are the following:

- Usually, eDonkey clients use the same software. If vulnerability exists on software, it means that the same vulnerability exists on all computers using that software.
- The shared files are huge. In classic architectures, worms are so small, that a single TCP segment can carry them. File size is not a restriction on P2P systems.
- eDonkey software runs on personal computers used by people who are far from expert in computer security. This increases vulnerability.
- Users rarely report security problems because of the illegal nature of the downloading.
- No worm detection mechanism is specified on eDonkey. In [16], Wei Yu et al. studied the impact of Peer-To-Peer systems on active worm propagation over Internet.

Their main goal was to develop an analytical methodology that can be used qualitatively to better understand the worm's impact using P2P on the Internet. Simulation showed that a P2P system can be a vehicle for the active worm attacker to achieve fast propagation. In this paper, P2P worm propagation strategies are classified as follows:

1. Pure Random-based scan (PRS): in this strategy, the P2P worm behaves as in classic networks. It selects an IP address randomly and tries to jump to it.
2. Offline P2P based Hitlist Scan (OPHLS): in this strategy, the worm collects IP addresses by acceding to the overlay routing table of its first victim. Thereafter, the worm jumps to these addresses following a tree scheme. Each time the worm reaches a new victim, it divides the Hitlist for each duplicate. This mechanism is used recurrently until the last machine in the Hitlist is reached. For the best propagation, this worm can use the PRS strategy to infect new victims.
3. Online P2P Scan (OPS): this strategy is similar to the previous one. The only difference is that the client to which the worm will jump must be connected to the P2P network. In OPHLS, this condition does not exist. The worm uses its capacity to reach the maximum number of peer neighbours. If total capacity is not reached, it can propagate with the PRS strategy.

To our knowledge, there have been no reports concerning worms on the eDonkey network. As soon as a new vulnerability is discovered, new malicious software (e.g. worms, virus...) exploiting this vulnerability appear. So we forecast the emergence of new worms which will take advantage of eDonkey network features. The OPS strategy could play the role of an accelerator vector for the propagation of those worms.

2.2. *The Sybil Attack*

The Sybil attack [3], involves creating several identities for one entity over the P2P network. This attack does not have an important security impact, but it can be used as a first step for other attacks (eclipse attack). To prevent this attack, it is reported [6] that an eDonkey server accepts a maximum of 3 client connections from the same IP address. This is not sufficient, an attacker can bypass it by possessing a large number of IP addresses. If it succeeds, this attack has one of the following impacts:

- By registering a high number of clients, an attacker makes a server refuse future legitimate connection requests. Thus, it creates a DoS situation on the eDonkey network. An eDonkey network may be disrupted if a Sybil attack is launched against all its servers.
- For each identity, the attacker shares a large number of files. This forces the server to use all its CPU resources when refreshing its list of shared files.

Some researchers are interested in the Sybil attack, but they often investigate structured P2P systems. The Sybil attack is still an open research topic in unstructured P2P systems like eDonkey.

2.3. *The Eclipse Attack*

The eclipse attack is closely related to the Sybil attack [8,9]. It involves controlling strategic nodes over the P2P network. By launching it, an attacker subdivides a virtual network, and eavesdrops on communications between partitions. An eclipse attack has more impact on hybrid P2P overlays, because of super-nodes, which are more important than other nodes. Existing research work is being conducted more on structured and hybrid than on unstructured P2P systems.

Eclipse is an overlay attack; it disrupts both P2P functionality and the sublevels network (IP routing). This attack is our starting point for our contributions in the next section. Some eDonkey attacks, such as flow redirection attack, are similar to the Eclipse attack. To accomplish redirection attack, an attacker needs to control at least one server. Upon receiving client requests, the malicious server replies with an IP's victim machine as a source. These replies do not take into consideration the keywords mentioned by clients. Thus, a Distributed Denial of Service attack is generated against the victim machine.

2.4. *Malwares*

Malware is a combination of two words, malicious and software. It refers to a file that contains a virus, backdoors or a security-compromising program. Malwares are very active on the eDonkey network. Users rarely scan downloaded files, and do not suspect a file simply by referring to its size, because several video/audio extensions are used. Furthermore, viruses can be split over several file blocks, and become active wherever the file is reassembled. Thus, they become more difficult to detect. In [5], authors tested two popular file sharing systems: limeware (gnutella) and OpenFT (FastTrack). Their test consisted of scanning a huge number of downloaded files using ClamAV: a free virus analyser. The test required 45 days and gave the following results:

- No less than 68% of archived and compressed files were malicious on Gnutella. On FastTrack, the percentage was 3% for malicious files.
- 99% of malicious files detected on Gnutella contained only 3 different malicious codes. On FastTrack, 75% of malicious files were using 3 different codes.
- On Gnutella, 28% of malicious sources had Private IP addresses. On FastTrack, a single IP address shared 67% of the downloaded malicious files.

A client sharing a Malware does not necessarily know that it is malicious; usually, users share malicious files without scanning them and are unaware of their malicious effect.

2.5. *Poisoning files*

A poisoning file is a file providing a content that does not match its description. It usually describes a recent and popular movie or video clip. On eDonkey, this phenomenon is often observed. The more client A downloads from client B, the faster client B will download from client A. Attackers use poisoning files in order to download their desired files faster, because of the popularity of their shared files.

This attack does not have a critical impact, but it can overload the P2P overlay and the ISP infrastructure. eMule offers a feature which works only with videos. This feature is a previewing file, which can be used to verify whether the downloaded file is poisoned or not, by viewing the first minutes of a downloaded movie. This solution is limited because the client has to download the first blocks before the rest, which is not always possible with eDonkey. Sequential block downloading is not necessary using eMule.

3. Topology Change Attacks Scenarios

In this section, we present some scenarios leading to a topology change attack. Detailed scenarios are specific to the eDonkey application. The topology change attack can be seen as an Eclipse attack. In a topology change attack, the final objective is to redirect communications towards all or part of a specific targeted network, rather than eavesdropping. In our scenario examples, we consider an ISP infrastructure as the targeted network. Topology change attack has one or more of the following impacts:

- eDonkey servers overload, disrupting all the P2P system. Consequently, ISP segments become overloaded.
- ISP equipment (routers) overload, implying congestion problems and crashes in extreme cases.
- P2P and ISP performance decrease. Scenarios are classified according to the technique used to accomplish them. In most of the scenarios, the attacker must control one or more eDonkey servers to launch a Topology change attack. The techniques are: server-list priority change, server-list alteration, server-list filtering modification.

3.1. *Using server-list priority change*

For eDonkey clients, a priority is assigned for each server: low, medium or high. The higher the server priority is, the higher the probability of receiving a connection request. This technique consists of modifying the priority. The interest of doing this for an attacker is to make malicious or controlled servers popular. The attacker does not need to control a server.

- *Scenario 1*: In this scenario, the attacker sets a legitimate eDonkey server to high priority and sets the others to low priority. The ISP hosting the server is the targeted infrastructure. *Effect:* a large number of connection requests are received by the server. *Objective:* to overload the ISP infrastructure by generating a huge amount of client-server communications.
- Scenario 2: Similar to scenario1, except that the attacker sets more than one controlled server to high priority. When receiving search requests, malicious servers reply with a malicious list of sources. The attacker selects only sources hosted on the targeted ISP. *Effect:* All download flows are redirected to the ISP infrastructure. *Objective:* to overload the targeted ISP with a huge download flow.
- Scenario 3: The attacker runs malicious servers over the targeted infrastructure. Thereafter, he sets them to high priority. *Effect:* both signalling and download flows are redirected to the targeted ISP. *Objective:*

overload the ISP infrastructure with client-client and client-server communications.

3.2. *Using server-list alteration*

The attacker does not modify server priority; instead, he modifies the server-list by adding or removing servers. We assume here that S is an eDonkey server.

- *Scenario 4:* Consists of adding or removing S from the server-list, S has low priority. *Effect:* no effect on the ISP infrastructure.
- *Scenario 5:* The attacker adds S, which has a high level priority, to the server-list. *Effect:* the same as in scenarios 2,3.
- *Scenario 6:* The attacker removes high priority S from the server- list. *Effect:* the same effect as for scenarios 1, 2,3 if all non-malicious servers are removed.

3.3. *Using modification of Server-List filter*

This technique involves modification of eDonkey clients' ip-filter.dat. By adding S to this list, the attacker makes S invisible and S client connections shut down. These clients reinitiate connections to visible servers. If the attacker removes S from this list, S become visible and able to receive connection requests.

- *Scenario 7:* Adding or removing S from the ip-filter list. S has a low priority. *Effect:* no effect on the ISP infrastructure.
- *Scenario 8:* In this scenario, the attacker adds S to the list. S has a high level priority. *Effect:* the same as for scenarios 1, 2 and 3 if S is not malicious.
- *Scenario 9:* In this scenario, the attacker removes S from the list. S has a high level priority. *Effect:* the same as for scenarios 1, 2 and 3 if S is not malicious.

4. Topology Change Attack Cases

In this section, we classify preview scenarios in a few attack cases. The measure considered in this classification is the nature of the redirected flow: signalling flow, downloading, or both of them.

4.1. *Topology change attack by redirecting signal flow*

This case considers client-server communications. All or part of the signalling flow is deviated towards the targeted ISP. The impact of such an attack is very dangerous, especially, for ISP infrastructures. On eDonkey, client-server connections are kept open for the whole session. This fact worsens the impact.

In order to succeed, this attack requires as a first step the success of one of the following attacks: setting all servers hosted on the targeted ISP to high priority level and the others to low priority and removing all servers not hosted on the targeted ISP from the server-list.

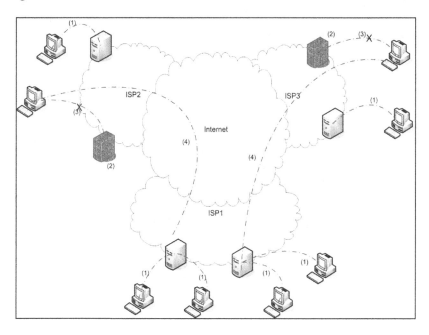

Figure 1. Example of signalling flow Topology Change Attack

Figure 1 shows a typical example of redirecting signal flow. It illustrates three ISPs (ISP1, ISP2, ISP3) interconnected over the Internet. Each ISP hosts eDonkey clients and servers. The signalling flow is represented by a discontinuous red line and, the download flow by a continuous blue line. For clarity's sake, we assume that the two parts of a client-server communication are hosted on the same ISP. In fact this is very close to reality. 1) In this example, two client-server communications are considered. 2) The attack makes non-ISP1 servers invisible to their clients. 3) The attack breaks these flows down by inserting, into the list-filter, the IP address of a server which does not belong to ISP1. 4) These clients will initiate new connections to ISP1 servers. When this attack is launched, a huge number of clients will reinitiate connections to servers hosted by ISP1. Client-server communications will then overload the ISP1 infrastructure. Therefore, this attack is considered as a "Topology Change Attack".

4.2. *Topology change attack by redirecting downloading flow*

We consider here client-client communications. This attack concentrates a large amount of downloading transfers from clients hosted by the targeted ISP, and requires malicious server setting. The servers' role is to reply to search requests from a malicious source list as shown in the eclipse attack in section III. All sources of the malicious list must be hosted on the targeted ISP.

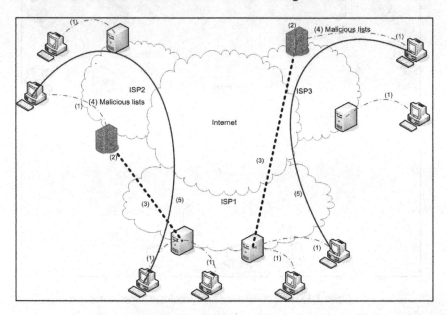

Figure 2. Example of download flow Topology Change Attack

Figure 2 illustrates an example of this case using the same network scheme as in figure 1. The signalling flow is represented by a discontinuous red line and, the download flow by a continuous blue line. 1) We assume that the two parts of a client-server communication are hosted by the same ISP. 2) The first step for an attacker is to hijack eDonkey servers and make them malicious. Malicious servers act as legitimate clients for the ISP1. 3) When receiving a search request for a file F, a malicious server forwards it to an ISP1 server. The ISP1 server will then reply with a list of ISP1 sources sharing the file F. Upon receiving this list, 4) the malicious server forwards it to the client that initiated the research request. Recognising only ISP1 sources, 5) this client will download the F blocks from ISP1 clients only. Successful initiation of this attack results in a dramatic impact on ISP1.

4.3. *Topology change attack by redirecting signalling and downloading flows*

This attack is the combination of both of the previous cases. It has a higher impact compared with a single attack, because both client-client and client-server communications are redirected toward the targeted ISP.

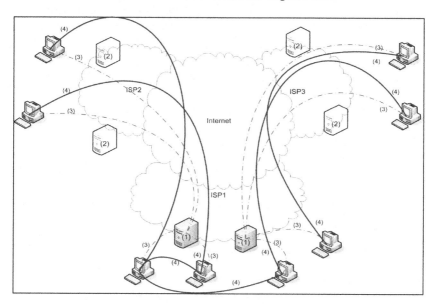

Figure 3. Example of signalling and download flows Topology Change Attack

Figure 3 illustrates this attack using the same scheme as figure 1. The signalling flow is represented by a discontinuous red line and the data flow by a continuous blue line. 1) The attack needs to set ISP1 servers only to visible and 2) make the rest invisible. The non-ISP1 servers may be rendered invisible by inserting them into the list-filter. The greater the number of modified client lists, the more dangerous the impact. 3) Recognising only ISP1 servers, a client can make a reconnection only to one of these. Once this step is accomplished, all the signalling flow over the eDonkey network will transit by the ISP1 infrastructure, thus overloading it. Furthermore, if the ISP1 servers are hijacked, they may reply to research requests with only source lists hosted on ISP1. 4) So, at least one of the two clients in a download communication is hosted by ISP1. Now, both signalling and data flows transit through the ISP1 infrastructure.

Since it is receiving all the eDonkey flow, the ISP infrastructure may be badly overloaded and congested.

5. Conclusion

We have presented the Topology Change Attack against a P2P network. The application studied is eDonkey because it is popular and used massively. By taking into account its architecture and functioning, we have defined all possible scenarios that can lead to a Topology change Attack. Such an attack can be a signal redirection, a data flow redirection or both. This attack can disrupt all of the P2P system, in most cases causing DoS on eDonkey servers. Network layers are strongly dependent, especially routing and overlay ones. If one of them is under attack, other layers are affected too. The main objective here is to demonstrate that a Topology change Attack has an overlay impact which can disrupt or crash the whole infrastructure.

References

1. ANDROUTSELLIS-THEOTOKIS, S., AND SPINELLIS, D. A survey of peer-to-peer content distribution technologies. ACM Comput. Surv. 36, 4 (2004), 335–371.
2. CHEN, Z., GAO, L., AND KWIAT, K. Modeling the spread of active worms, 2003.
3. DOUCEUR, J. R. The sybil attack. In IPTPS' 01: Revised Papers from the First International Workshop on Peer-to-Peer Systems (London, UK, 2002), Springer-Verlag, pp. 251–260.
4. HANDURUKANDE, S. B., KERMARREC, A.-M., FESSANT, F. L., MASSOULI'E , L., AND PATARIN, S. Peer sharing behaviour in the edonkey network, and implications for the design of server-less file sharing systems. SIGOPS Oper. Syst. Rev. 40, 4 (2006), 359–371.
5. KALAFUT, A., ACHARYA, A., AND GUPTA, M. A study of Malware in peer-to-peer networks. In IMC '06: Proceedings of the 6th ACM SIGCOMM on Internet measurement (New York, NY, USA, 2006), ACM Press, pp. 327–332.
6. KULBAK Y. and BICKSON D.: The eMule protocol specification (January 2005), the Hebrew University of Jerusalem, Jerusalem.
7. SEN, S., AND WANG, J. Analyzing peer-to-peer traffic across large networks. In IMW '02: Proceedings of the 2nd ACM SIGCOMM Workshop on Internet measurment (New York, NY, USA, 2002), ACM Press, pp. 137–150.
8. SINGH, A., CASTRO, M., DRUSCHEL, P., AND ROW, A. Defending against eclipse attacks on overlay networks, 2004.
9. SINGH, A., NGAN, T.-W. J., DRUSCHEL, P., AND WALLACH, D. S. Eclipse attacks on overlay networks: Threats and defenses. In IEEE INFOCOM 2006 (Barcelona, Spain, Apr. 2006). To appear.

10. TUTSCHKU, K. A measurement-based traffic profile of the edonkey filesharing service. In 5th Passive and Active Measurement Workshop (PAM2004) (Antibes Juan-les-Pins, France. April 19-20., 4 2004).
11. YANG, J., MA, H., SONG, W., CUI, J., AND ZHOU, C. Crawling the edonkey network. In GCC Workshops (2006), pp. 133–136.
12. ZHOU, L., ZHANG, L., MCSHERRY, F., IMMORLICA, N., COSTA, M., AND CHIEN, S. A first look at peer-to-peer worms: Threats and defenses.
13. STOICA, I., MORRIS, R., KARGER, D., KAASHOEK, M.,AND BALAKRISHNAN, H. 2001. Chord: A scalable peer-to-peer lookup service for internet applications.In Proceedings of SIGCOMM 2001.
14. ROWSTRON, A. AND DRUSCHEL, P. 2001. Pastry: Scalable, distributed object location and routing for large-scale peer-to-peer systems. In Proceedings of IFIP/ACMMiddleware. Heidelberg, Germany.
15. ZHAO, B., JOSEPH, A., AND KUBIATOWICZ, J. 2002. Locality aware mechanisms for large-scale networks. In Proceedings of the International Workshop on Future Directions in Distributed Computing (FuDiCo2002).
16. YU W., BOYER C., CHELLAPPAN S., and XUAN D. Peer-to-peer system-based active worm attacks: Modeling and analysis. In Proceedings of IEEE International Conference on Communications (ICC '05), pages 295--300, 2005.
17. Bittorrent, 2004. http://bitconjurer.org/BitTorrent/.

DEVICE PAIRING USING UNIDIRECTIONAL PHYSICAL CHANNELS[†]

NITESH SAXENA AND MD. BORHAN UDDIN

Polytechnic University,
nsaxena@duke.poly.edu, borhan@cis.poly.edu

"Pairing" is referred to as the operation of achieving authenticated key agreement between two human-operated devices over a short-range wireless communication channel (such as Bluetooth, WiFi). The devices are ad hoc in nature, i.e., they can neither be assumed to have a prior context with each other nor do they share a common trusted authority. However, the devices can generally be connected using auxiliary physical channel(s) (such as audio, visual, etc.) that can be authenticated by the device user(s), and thus form the basis for pairing.

Recently proposed pairing protocols are based upon bidirectional physical channels. However, in various pairing scenarios, only a unidirectional physical channel exists between two devices (such as between an access point and a cell phone). In this paper, we consider pairing devices using a unidirectional physical channel and focus on a recently proposed protocol on this topic by Saxena *et al.* [13]. As an improvement to [13], we present an efficient implementation of a physical channel based on multiple LEDs as transmitters and a video camera as a receiver.

1. Introduction

Short-range wireless communication, based on technologies such as Bluetooth and WiFi, is becoming increasingly popular and promises to remain so in the future. With this surge in popularity, come various security risks. Wireless communication channel is easy to eavesdrop upon and to manipulate, and therefore a fundamental security objective is to secure this communication channel. In this paper, we will use the term "pairing" to refer to the operation of bootstrapping secure communication between two devices connected with a short-range wireless channel. The examples of pairing, from day-to-day life, include pairing of a WiFi laptop and an access point, a Bluetooth keyboard and a desktop, and so on. Pairing would be easy to achieve if there existed a global infrastructure enabling devices to share an on- or off-line trusted third party, a certification authority, a PKI or any pre-configured secrets. However, such a

---

[†] A fuller version of this paper is available at [20]

global infrastructure is close to impossible to come by in practice, thereby making pairing an interesting and a challenging real-world research problem.

A recent research direction to pairing is to use an auxiliary physically authenticatable channel i.e., physical channel, also called an out-of-band (OOB) channel, which is governed by humans, i.e., by the users operating the devices. Examples of OOB channels include audio, visual channels, etc. Unlike the wireless channel, on the OOB channel, an adversary is assumed to be incapable of modifying messages, however, it can eavesdrop on them. A pairing scheme should therefore be secure against such an adversary.

The usability of a pairing scheme based on OOB channels is clearly of utmost importance. Since the OOB channels typically have low bandwidth, the shorter the data that a pairing scheme needs to transmit over these channels, the better the scheme becomes in terms of usability.

Various pairing protocols have been proposed so far. These protocols are generally based on the **bidirectional** automated device-to-device (d2d) OOB channels. Such d2d channels require both devices to have transmitters and the corresponding receivers.

An earlier pairing protocol [1] requires at least 160 to 80 bits of data to be transmitted over the OOB channels. The more recent, so-called SAS- (Short Authenticated Strings) based protocols, [7], [9], reduce the length of data to be transmitted over the OOB channels to only 15 bits or so.[‡]

Based on the above protocols, a number of pairing schemes with various OOB channels have been proposed. We review these in the next section. In this paper, we concentrate on pairing devices using **unidirectional** OOB channels. The motivation for this is that in various pairing scenarios bidirectional d2d channels do not exist because only one of the devices being paired has a receiver such as while pairing WiFi laptop and a cell phone. Since receivers are generally expensive, it is not feasible to add them onto commodity devices, such as access points, Bluetooth headsets, etc. Moreover, even in scenarios, where bidirectional d2d do exist, it is always beneficial to use only one of them for efficiency and usability reasons.

With the above motivation, we focus on a pairing method that can be used for pairing two devices using a "short" unidirectional OOB channel in one direction and a unidirectional "single-bit" OOB channel in the other direction [13]. Since a "single-bit" channel is easy and fast to implement, we ignore this bi-directionality and from here on, refer to the protocol of [13] as a protocol that can pair two devices using a unidirectional OOB channel.

[‡]The concept of SAS-based authentication was first introduced by Vaudenay in [17].

Our Contribution. In this paper, as an improvement to [13], we propose a new implementation of an OOB channel using multiple LEDs as transmitter and video camera as receiver. Unlike the results of [13], the implementation of our channel is much more efficient and its bandwidth improves with the increase in the number of LEDs. Since most devices have multiple LEDs (and if not, they can be cheaply added on), our implementation is an efficient way to pair two devices (such as headset and camera phone, access point and camera phone, etc.), one of which has a video camera. Our implementation has other useful applications in Bluetooth/WiFi device discovery, sensor network key distribution and in general, for low-bandwidth data transmission.

Organization. The rest of the paper is organized as follows. In Section 2, we review the prior pairing schemes. In Section 3, we describe the security model and summarize relevant protocols. In Section 4, we discuss the design, implementation and performance of our implementation of a d2d channel using LEDs and video camera.

2. Related Work

There exists a significant amount of prior work on the general topic of pairing. Due to space constraints we only summarize it here.

Balfanz, *et al.* [1] proposed pairing using infrared as a d2d channel; the devices exchange their public keys over the wireless channel, then exchange (at least 80-bit long) hashes of their respective public keys over the infrared channel.

The Snowflake mechanism by Levienet *et al.* [5] and the Random Arts visual hash by Perrig *et al.* [10], can be used for pairing devices based on comparison of random images.

McCune *et al.* proposed the "Seeing-is-Believing" (SiB) scheme [8]. SiB involves establishing two unidirectional visual d2d channels; one device encodes the data into a two-dimensional barcode and the other device reads it using a still camera.

Goodrich, *et al.* [6] proposed a pairing scheme based on "Mad Lib" sentences that is also built upon the protocol of Balfanz *et al.* The main idea of their procedure is to encode the pairing data into English sentences, which users can compare easily.

As an improvement to SiB [8], Saxena *et al.* [13] proposed a new scheme based on visual OOB channel. This is the scheme that we analyze and improve upon in this paper. The scheme uses one of the SAS protocols [7] [9], and is aimed at pairing two devices (such as a cell phone and an access point), only one of which has a relevant receiver (such as a camera). The protocol is described in more detail in Section 3.

A very recent proposal [15] focuses on pairing two devices with the help of "button presses" by the user. This scheme is based upon a protocol that first performs an unauthenticated Diffie-Hellman key agreement, then authenticates the established key using a short password. Such a short password can be agreed upon between the two devices via three protocol variants that make use of button presses.

3. Communication and Security Model, and Applicable Protocols

The pairing protocols are based upon the following communication and adversarial model [17]. The devices being paired are connected via two types of channels: (1) a short-range, high-bandwidth bidirectional wireless channel, and (2) low-bandwidth OOB channel(s). Based on device types, the OOB channel(s) can be device-to-device (d2d), device-to-human (d2h) and/or human-to-device (h2d). An adversary attacking the pairing protocol is assumed to have full control on the wireless channel, namely, it can eavesdrop, delay, drop, replay and modify messages. On the OOB channel, the adversary can eavesdrop messages; however, it can not modify them. In other words, the OOB channel is assumed to be an authenticated channel.

To date, two three-round pairing protocols based on short authenticated strings (SAS) have been proposed [9], [7]. The SAS protocol variant of [13] can be based on both of these protocols. In a communication setting involving two users restricted to running three instances of the protocol, these protocols need to transmit only k (= 15) bits of data over the OOB channels. As long as the cryptographic primitives used in the protocols are secure, an adversary attacking these protocols can not win with a probability significantly higher than 2^{-k} (= 2^{-15}). This gives us security equivalent to the security provided by 5-digit PIN-based ATM authentication.

4. Pairing with a Unidirectional OOB Channel

In this paper, we focus upon pairing scenarios where bidirectional OOB channels do not exist. To this end, we consider the protocol of Saxena et al. [13], which requires a unidirectional OOB channel. The protocol works as follows. Over the wireless channel, A and B follow the underlying SAS protocol. Then a unidirectional OOB channel is established by device A transmitting the SAS data. This is followed by device B comparing the received data with its own copy of the SAS data, and transmitting the resulting bit b of comparison over a OOB channel (say, displayed on its screen). Finally, the user reads the transmitted bit *b* and accordingly indicates the result to device A. The unidirectional d2d channel was implemented using a single blinking LED as a transmitter and a video camera as a receiver.

In this paper, as an improvement to [13], we propose a new implementation of an OOB channel using multiple LEDs as transmitter and video camera as receiver. Unlike the results of [13], the implementation of our channel is much more efficient and its bandwidth improves with the increase in the number of LEDs. Since most devices have multiple LEDs (and if not, they can be cheaply added on), our implementation is an efficient way to pair two devices (such as headset and camera phone, access point and camera phone, etc.), one of which has a video camera. The implementation can also be used on regular displays by simulating the LEDs on them.

In the rest of this section, we discuss the design, implementation and performance of our implementation. We also discuss the applications of our implementation in Bluetooth/WiFi device discovery, sensor network key distribution and in general, for low-bandwidth data transmission.

4.1. *Encoding using LEDs*

In our encoding, we need two types of LEDs: a "sync" LED (red color LED) for synchronization at the beginning and end of SAS data transmission, and one or more "data" LEDs (green color LEDs) for transmitting the SAS data. The sync LED is used for indicating the beginning and end of the SAS data transmission in order to detect any synchronization delays, adversarial or otherwise, between the two devices. The sync LED is kept in "ON" state only at the beginning and end of data transmission and in "OFF" state otherwise.

The data LEDs are used for SAS data transmission by indicating different bits ('0'/'1') for different states (OFF/ON) of LEDs. If N is the number of Data LEDs, the transmitter can display N bits of SAS data at a time. The states of the sync and data LEDs are kept unchanged for a certain time period (named "hold time"; experimentally determined as 300ms); so that, a stable state (named "BitFrame") can be easily captured in the video stream of the receiver video camera. After every 300 ms, next N bits of the SAS data are shown in the next frame. This process continues until all bits of SAS data are transmitted. If the last frame does not have N number of SAS bits to show, the beginning required LEDs show the data bits and the remaining are kept OFF.

For discovering the LEDs' location, color, dimension at the receiver side, we need two extra frames at the beginning of transmission– an "All-ON" frame having all LEDs in ON state and an "All-OFF" frame having all LEDs in OFF state. In addition to All-ON and All-OFF frames, we need another frame at the end of SAS data transmission, to detect synchronization delays, having the sync LED in ON state and the data LEDs in OFF state. Thus, the total number of frames to be transmitted for 15-bit SAS is $\lceil 15/N \rceil + 3$, which yields a total transmission time of $[\lceil 15/N \rceil + 3] * 300$ ms, where N is the number of data LEDs.

4.2. Decoding using a Video Camera

The two devices being paired first execute the protocol of [13] over the wireless channel. After that the receiver turns on its video camera, asks the user to adjust its camera setting and focus on the LED-based display of the transmitting device and press "OK" button when done. When the user completes the steps, the receiver sends the "ready" signal to the transmitter and requests the transmitter to send the acknowledgement over the wireless channel when it is done with computing its SAS value and ready to start transmitting over the unidirectional channel. The transmitter does the steps and all the frames are captured maintaining the synchronization of Figure 1. In this figure, each small rectangle on the receiving window denotes a video frame of video stream and brown arrow marked with "Video Stream Capturing" denotes the propagation of transmitted signal to streamed frame in video stream, which makes sense that there is some propagation delay of an input transition from transmitter's side to receiver's video stream.

4.2.1. Detection of LEDs and Retrieval of SAS data from Video Frames

The frames are processed after the completion of capturing of all transmitted frames. From All-OFF and All-ON frames LEDs location, dimension and color are detected. Rests of the frames are used for retrieving SAS data and synchronization test.

Our LEDs location and dimension detection algorithm is a simple but fast, robust and efficient one - unlike any existing object/face detection algorithms [11, 18, 12]. It detects the position and dimension of LEDs deterministically. It is able to detect any shape/geometry of LEDs unlike [18, 12] and doesn't require any prior training unlike [11, 18]. It uses the color threshold adjustment technique like [19] to detect the LEDs position and dimension.

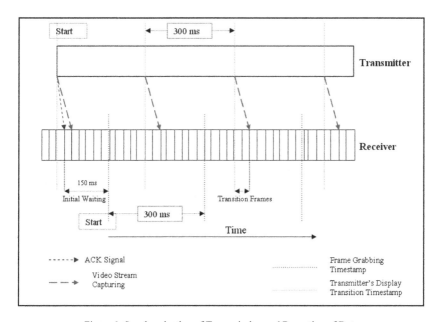

Figure 1: Synchronization of Transmission and Reception of Data

The maximal differences of RGB values, i.e. *max(dR, dG, dB)* of each pixel of All-OFF and All-ON frames are measured and kept in memory, and using a threshold value for *max(dR, dG, dB)*, BitStrings are built for each row of pixel.

From the BitStrings, LEDs location, dimension is discovered and count of LEDs is determined; and count of discovered LEDs is matched against the original count of the LEDs. This process continues up to a number of times by adjusting the threshold value of *max(dR, dG, dB)* and constructing the new bit strings until the discovered count of LEDs matches with original count.

After successful discovery of LEDs, dimension, average RGB values of ON and OFF states of LEDs area for each LEDs are stored in memory from All-OFF and All-ON frames for detecting the On-Off state of LEDs in subsequent BitFrames. SAS data is extracted by exploring the LEDs location in data frames.

Data frames are checked for the OFF state of the SYNC LED. The last frame is examined to determine whether the sync LED is in the ON state and that all data LEDs are in the OFF state. If the SYNC LED isn't in proper state, there is an indication of a sync failure due to synchronization delays. If the extracted SAS matches with the computed SAS on the receiver and the frames pass the synchronization test, the receiver and transmitter are successfully paired. Otherwise, they fail due to mismatch of SAS or delay in synchronization.

For a successful pairing, the LEDs are marked with a rectangle of green color around them; and for a failed case, the LEDs are crossed with red color. Observing the graphical result on screen of the receiver, the user either accepts or aborts the pairing on the transmitter's device.

4.3. *Experimental Setup*

We implemented and tested our channel in two different settings. One showed the BitFrames on the monitor of a DELL desktop PC (Intel Xenon Processor 1.8 GHz with 1 GB RAM, WinXP SP2) and the other showed the BitFrames on real implementation of the scheme on breadboard using 7 LEDs (1 SYNC and 6 data LEDs), the breadboard is interfaced to the DELL desktop PC using DB-25 parallel port. In the first setting, bitmap images of actual ON and OFF states of real LEDs are used. The picture of transmitter in second setting is shown in Figure 2.

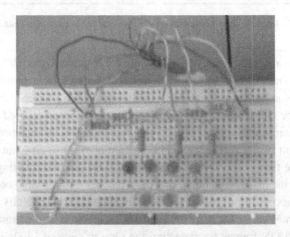

Figure 2: Transmitter-Breadboard with LEDs

In both the schemes receiver is the Dell Vostro1500 (Intel Core 2 Duo 1.6 GHz with 2 GB RAM, WinXP SP2) Laptop having Integrated Webcam (30 frames/second, frame size 640X480 pixels) and wireless channel is Wireless network of our university (54 Mbps). We wrote the simulator in Microsoft VC# to implement the last two OOB message transmissions as in the protocol of [13], and to construct and show the pairing result on receiver's screen. Client-server communication model over the wireless network is used for wireless communication between transmitter and receiver.

4.4. *Experiment Results*

From the result of the first setting, we found that our implementation works for different number and orientation of LEDs, different brightness of the monitor and different distance (less than 1.5–2 meters) between the transmitter and receiver. Our implementation in the second setting also works fine for scattered light from LEDs and up to 2.5 meters of distance, longer than in the first setting. Lights from LEDs directly falls on camera and thus ON-OFF state detection becomes easy as there is more change in lighting effect in this setting. Based on the results obtained, we summarize the following salient characteristics of our implementation in both the settings.

Transmission Time: Using N data LEDs and one sync LED, the transmission requires about $[\lceil 15/N \rceil +3]*300$ ms for 15-bits of SAS data. Extraction of SAS data from captured frames requires less than 1 second. Therefore, for a typical display which has 2 data LEDs and 1 sync LED, our scheme requires less than 4.15 seconds to complete the whole process.

Distance: Our schemes work well if the distance between the sender and receiver is less than 1.5-2.5 meters. This represents a promising improvement over the existing d2d channels as [13], which can work for very little distance between the transmitter and receiver.

Brightness and Intensity of Light: Our channel is robust to varying brightness and intensity of light. It compares the states of LEDs ON and OFF state on current default settings of brightness and intensity of light on devices we tested on. From first two, All-OFF and All-ON frames, it learns the environment in online.

4.5. *Other Applications of Our Implementation*

In addition to pairing, our implementation has other applications, as follows.

Device Discovery: A device needs to, before starting to communicate with another wireless device, first determine its address. Currently, in Bluetooth and WiFi, such a device discovery is slow and tedious for the users to perform as there might be a number of devices in the neighborhood. Using our d2d channel, one can perform device discovery over the physical channel itself. Using just two data LEDs, it would only take about 9 seconds to discover a 48-bit long Bluetooth device address, and ease the burden on the user.

Secure Key Distribution in Sensor Networks: Before deploying a sensor network, the nodes need to be provided with keys that they can use to secure communicate among themselves. Due to the lack of a trusted infrastructure and interfaces (such as USB) on sensors, such a key distribution needs to be performed on-site wirelessly by the administrator of the network. We are currently in the process of extending our implementation of the d2d channel and to simultaneously pair each sensor node with the base station. Most existing commercial sensor nodes generally have three LEDs and the base station PC can be easily connected with a web camera. We believe that our approach would be much more efficient, scalable and usable than a recently proposed scheme [3].

General Data Transmission: Our implementation can also be used in applications other than security, for low-bandwidth data transmission. Using N data LEDs (or an equivalent sized display) and a hold time of 300 ms, we are able to achieve a bandwidth of 3.33N bps. With such a bandwidth, one could efficiently send out information such as advertisements, calendars, low-resolution images, etc.

5. Conclusion

In this paper, we focused upon pairing two devices using unidirectional OOB channels. We devised an efficient implementation of an OOB channel using multiple LEDs as transmitter and video camera as a receiver. With a display consisting of just two LEDs, our implementation takes less than 6.5 seconds. With increase in the number of LEDs, the bandwidth of our channel gets better. For example, with six LEDs, we need less than 2.8 seconds. Our implementation has other useful applications in Bluetooth/WiFi device discovery, sensor network key distribution and in general for data transmission.

References

1. D. Balfanz, D. Smetters, P. Stewart, and H. C. Wong. Talking to strangers: Authentication in ad-hoc wireless networks. In NDSS, 2002.
2. R. Canetti and H. Krawczyk. Analysis of key-exchange protocols and their use for building secure channels. In EUROCRYPT, 2001.
3. K. Cynthia, M. Luk, R. Negi, and A. Perrig. Message-in-a-bottle: User-friendly and secure key deployment for sensor nodes. In ACM SenSys-2007.
4. W. Du, J. Deng, Y. S. Han, and P. K. Varshney. A pairwise key pre-distribution scheme for wireless sensor networks. In ACM CCS, 2003.
5. I. Goldberg. Visual Key Fingerprint Code, 1996. Available at http://www.cs.berkeley.edu/iang/visprint.c

6. M. T. Goodrich, M. Sirivianos, J. Solis, G. Tsudik, and E. Uzun. Loud and Clear: Human-Verifiable Authentication Based on Audio. In ICDCS, 2006.

7. S. Laur, N. Asokan, and K. Nyberg. Efficient mutual data authentication based on short authenticated strings. IACR Cryptology ePrint Archive: Report 2005/424, 2005.

8. J. M. McCune, A. Perrig, and M. K. Reiter. Seeing-is-believing: Using camera phones for human-verifiable authentication. In IEEE Symposium on Security and Privacy, 2005.

9. S. Pasini and S. Vaudenay. SAS-Based Authenticated Key Agreement. In PKC, 2006.

10. A. Perrig and D. Song. Hash visualization: a new technique to improve real-world security. In CrypTEC, 1999.

11. H. A. Rowley, S. Baluja, and T. Kanade. Neural network-based face detection. In Pattern Analysis and Machine Intelligence (PAMI), 1998.

12. K. Sandeep and A. Rajagopalan. Human face detection in cluttered color images using skin color and edge information. In Indian Conference on Computer Vision, Graphics and Image Processing (ICVGIP), 2002.

13. N. Saxena, J.-E. Ekberg, K. Kostiainen, and N. Asokan. Secure device pairing based on a visual channel. In IEEE Symposium on Security and Privacy (ISP'06), short paper, 2006.

14. F. Stajano and R. J. Anderson. The resurrecting duckling: Security issues for ad-hoc wireless networks. In Security Protocols Workshop, 1999.

15. C. Soriente, G. Tsudik, and E.~Uzun. BEDA: Button-Enabled Device Association. In IWSSI Worhshop, 2007.

16. J. Suomalainen, J. Valkonen, and N. Asokan. Security associations in personal networks: A comparative analysis. In ESAS, 2007.

17. S. Vaudenay. Secure communications over insecure channels based on short authenticated strings. In CRYPTO, 2005.

18. P. Viola and M. Jones. Rapid object detection using a boosted cascade of simple features. In Computer Vision and Pattern Recognition,2001.

19. J. Weszka. A survey of threshold selection techniques. In Computer Graphics and Image Processing. Vol. 7, 1978, pp. 259-265.

20. N. Saxena and B. Uddin. Device Pairing using Unidirectional Physical Channels. http://cis.poly.edu/~nsaxena/docs/su08.pdf

AN INDUSTRIAL AND ACADEMIC JOINT EXPERIMENT ON AUTOMATED VERIFICATION OF A SECURITY PROTOCOL

OLIVIER HEEN

IRISA, Lande Project, Rennes, France

THOMAS GENET

IRISA, Lande Project, Rennes, France

STEPHANE GELLER

ENS Cachan, Rennes, France

NICOLAS PRIGENT

Thomson R&D France, Security Lab, Rennes, France

This paper relates the collaboration between industrial and academic teams for the design and the verification of a security protocol. The protocol is about trust establishment in large communities of devices where infrastructure components are not always reachable. The collaboration covers the writing of formal specifications up to their verification, using both manual and automated verification methods embedded in the AVISPA [1] and SPAN [7] tools. At each stage, the use of the visualization and protocol animation facilities of SPAN is key to the mutual understanding of working teams. As a result, we obtain much more confidence in the security of the final protocol. We also demonstrate the usefulness of some embedded countermeasures.

1. Introduction

As they expand, digital transmissions require increased security. Sometimes a straightforward adaptation of widely known solutions (SSL, IPSEC, PGP...) is adequate. Sometimes a new protocol must be specifically designed. In this case, many sources of error exist:

- The protocol is an answer to a recent security problem: all the aspects of the problem may already not be known.
- The protocol is an answer to a time critical situation: the design time may be very short.

- The protocol is designed for commercial use in a competitive domain: some details may not be published too early, and thus no external review is possible.

Because of such error factors there is an urge need for formal verification. Moreover, if the formal verification can be automated, this gives a chance to systematically verify the protocol after each update and to deal with the complexity of some protocols that cannot be managed by hand in practice.

This paper relates the collaboration of industrial and academic teams about specifying and verifying one protocol. For convenience in the rest of the paper, we call our protocol LCDP for *Large Community of Device Protocol*. It is an adaptation of a symmetric key authentication scheme [4] to the case of large communities of devices. This collaboration illustrates the advantages of formal verification from a practical point of view: at first, it leads to a more precise specification of LCDP; then it gives more confidence on the final version, since no tools found attacks. This is especially true for the parts of the protocol that are completely new, and thus not heavily reviewed. At last, we check downgraded versions of LCDP where some countermeasures are disabled: this leads to the discovering of non-trivial attacks, and thus provides better justifications for the chosen countermeasures.

At each stage (formal specification, modeling, verification), the visualization and the interactive use of execution diagrams is key for the mutual understanding of both teams: the industrial team developing the LCDP, and the academic team leading the formal specification and verification effort. Throughout the paper, we provide some of the message sequence charts obtained with SPAN.

The section 2 gives the basics of automated protocol verification in the Dolev-Yao model. The tools that we use are also described. The section 3 gives motivations for LCDP and its description. The section 4 relates the whole verification process.

2. About automated protocol verification

This section is a short introduction to the automated verification of protocols in the Dolev-Yao model (that was introduced in [5]). The reader familiar with automated protocol verification can skip this section.

2.1. *Verification of Diffie-Hellman*

We briefly introduce the verification on a well-known example: the Diffie-Hellman key agreement protocol [6]. It is presented below, using the so-called

"Alice & Bob" notation. The agents are denoted by A and B and the established key is denoted by K. This key is used in the final step to encrypt a secret message msg sent by A to B.

1. $A \rightarrow B$: g^{Na}
2. $B \rightarrow A$: g^{Nb}, A and B compute key $K=(g^{Na})^{Nb}=(g^{Nb})^{Na}$
3. $A \rightarrow B$: $\{msg\}_K$

At step 1, A generates the *nonce* (a random number) N_a and computes g^{Na} where g is a public number. Then A sends g^{Na} to the agent B. At step 2, the agent B also generates a number N_b and computes g^{Nb} and $K=(g^{Na})^{Nb}$. The former is sent to A and the latter stands for the symmetric key shared between A and B.

As soon as A receives g^{Nb} from B, it computes $(g^{Nb})^{Na}$ and considers it as the symmetric key shared with B. Indeed, according to the algebraic properties of the exponentiation, $K=(g^{Na})^{Nb}=(g^{Nb})^{Na}$. Finally, the message $\{Msg\}_K$ is sent by A to B in which Msg is a datum standing to be secret between A and B, and $\{\ \}_K$ denotes the use of a symmetric encryption algorithm using the key K.

Security protocols can be attacked in several ways. If the keys or the algorithms used for ciphering messages are not robust enough, the content of the messages can be obtained or modified by an attacker. Such attacks are more related to cryptanalysis and can generally be avoided with a careful choice of keys and algorithms when implementing the protocol. The attacks we are interested in are based on a malicious use of the protocol itself. The Dolev-Yao model is particularly well suited for this kind of attacks. The intruder can read, block, store, modify and send messages over the network. It is said that *the intruder is the network.*

Hereafter, we show the well known man-in-the-middle attack against the Diffie-Hellman protocol. The notation I(A) means that the intruder pretends to be A.

1. $A \rightarrow I$: g^{Na}
2. $I(A) \rightarrow B$: g^{Ni}
3. $B \rightarrow I$: g^{Nb}, B and I compute the key $K_{IB}=(g^{Ni})^{Nb}=(g^{Nb})^{Ni}$
4. $I(B) \rightarrow A$: g^{Ni}, A and I compute the key $K_{IA}=(g^{Ni})^{Na}=(g^{Na})^{Ni}$
5. $A \rightarrow I$: $\{Msg\}_{K_{IA}}$

Roughly, the intruder establishes two keys: $K_{IA}=(g^{Na})^{Ni}$ with A at Steps 1 and 4, and $K^{IB}=(g^{Nb})^{Ni}$ with B at Steps 2 and 3. He then acts as a proxy between A and B. At Step 5, the agent A sends the secret data to B using the key K_{IA} shared with the intruder. The intruder then extracts the secret data.

2.2. Verification tools

Due to the intrinsic complexity of real-life protocols, their formal verification is unlikely to be performed by hand. For instance, the Needham-Schroeder Public Key protocol [10] was proved correct by hand [3] though it revealed to be flawed [9] when carefully analyzed using formal methods.

The verification in the Dolev-Yao model has been implemented in several tools. The AVISPA framework [1] is one such tool. It is very convenient, especially when completed with SPAN [7] for the visualization and animation parts. AVISPA and SPAN both use formal specifications of the protocols, written in the language of AVISPA called HLPSL (High Level Protocol Specification Language). Hereafter is a specification of the Diffie-Hellman protocol using HLPSL.

```
role alice(A,B:agent, G:text, Snd,Rcv:channel(dy)) played_by A def=
    local State:nat, Na,Msg:text, X,K:message init State:=1
transition
1.  State=1 /\ Rcv(start) =|> State':=2 /\ Na':=new() /\ Snd(exp(G,Na'))
2.  State=2 /\ Rcv(X') =|> State':=3 /\ K':=exp(X',Na) /\ Msg':= new() /\
    Snd({Msg'}_K')
end role

role bob(B,A:agent, G:text, Snd,Rcv:channel(dy)) played_by B def=
    local State:nat, Y,K:message, Nb,Msg:text init State:=1
transition
1.  State=1 /\ Rcv(Y') =|> State':=2 /\ Nb':=new() /\ K':=exp(Y',Nb') /\
    Snd(exp(G,Nb'))
2.  State=2 /\ Rcv({Msg'}_K) =|> State':=3
end role
```

The specification is based on role descriptions, i.e. finite state automata, where transitions are fired when a message is sent or received. Contrary to ``Alice & Bob'' notation, HLPSL imposes explicit definition of roles, nonce generation, message emission and reception, etc. In HLPSL, =|> stands for the transition relation and /\ stands for the usual conjunction symbol. The HLPSL is based on a notation à la TLA where the meaning of a primed variable X' depends on the location of this variable. Indeed, if X' occurs in a message pattern of the left-hand side of a transition then a new value is obtained for X by matching the message pattern on received messages. Then this value is accessible by X' in the same transition.

Hereafter is an attack automatically found by one AVISPA tool called ATSE. Note that this attack is not the usual man-in-the-middle attack. We believe that this is due to ATSE providing the shortest attack first.

```
SUMMARY        UNSAFE
DETAILS        ATTACK_FOUND TYPED_MODEL
PROTOCOL       Diffie-Hellman.if
GOAL           Secrecy attack on (n2(Msg))
BACKEND        CL-AtSe
STATISTICS     [...]
ATTACK TRACE
  i -> (a,3): start
  (a,3) -> i: exp(g,n1(Na))
  i -> (a,3): g
  (a,3) -> i: {n2(Msg)}_(exp(g,n1(Na))) & Secret(n2(Msg),set_53);
              Add a to set_53; Add b to set_53;
```

Figure 1 is a visualization of the man-in-the-middle attack built using SPAN. Starting for the HLPSL specification, SPAN lets the operator choose any possible transition, until there is no more possible transition.

In figure 1, the operator has chosen a transition sequence that leads to the attack. See [2] for more details about the formal specification of the Diffie-Hellman protocol and its verification using AVISPA and SPAN.

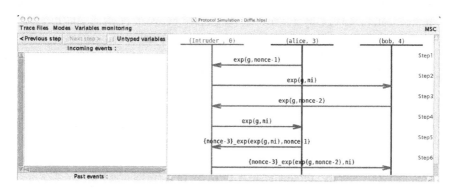

Figure 1: Visualization of the man in the middle attack with SPAN

3. Brief description of LCDP

This section describes LCDP and gives indication on how it was specified. The focus of the paper is the verification in section 4, but we first provide some rational for understanding LDCP. LCDP is meant to establish trust within large communities of devices. Here, the trust is the mutual authentication between community devices and, ultimately, the sharing of a secret key (as in [8] for instance). We believe that such communities will increasingly exist because of the generalization of cheap devices with network connectivity and the move towards ubiquitous computing [13]. In these communities the infrastructure components (internet server, home center, WiFi base…) are not always reachable, and thus should not be used often, in an opportunistic manner. One typical example is a cloud of home devices and personal devices willing to collaborate, but not always connected to a central home server. Moreover, the use of asymmetric cryptography on devices must be sparse because of their low computation capabilities. Refer to [8,11] for previous work by two authors on secure communities of devices.

3.1. *Symmetric key authentication*

LCDP is an adaptation of an existing symmetric key authentication scheme [4] in the case of large communities of devices. The principle is to allow devices to progressively acquire a set of trusted other devices. Once trust is established, devices can securely communicate on a one-to-one basis. To achieve this, LCDP uses a mix of several techniques and components. The components are: one authentication server, at least one directory server and the devices. The techniques are: Public Key Infrastructure (PKI) between devices and authentication server, symmetric cryptography between devices and directory servers, symmetric cryptography again between devices.

The notations used to describe LCDP are: AS for the authentication server, DS for the directory server, $D_1…D_i$ for devices having identities $Id_1…Id_i$ respectively.

In a typical session, a device D_1 first connects to AS, using its PKI credentials. If D_1 is authorized, then AS sends it a cryptographic ticket t_1. D_1 presents t_1 to DS in order to register. DS informs D_1 about other devices $\{D_i,…\}$ willing to communicate. For each D_i, DS also provides a specific ticket $t_{1,i}$. Only then may D_1 securely communicate with D_i by first presenting $t_{1,i}$.

3.2. *LCDP details*

The PKI part of LCDP can be a very common X509 architecture. The authentication server is typically a SSL server. It acts as a guard against non-authenticated devices. It also enforces the revocation of devices. The devices connect the authentication server only when they want to enter into a LCDP session. This happens typically once every day. Since we are in ad hoc context, we do not assume that the authentication server is always reachable. Moreover, the use of a PKI can be no more that opportunistic. For instance, the revocation information will be received by device only on a best effort basis.

The directory server is contacted by devices whenever they need references for other devices. This can happen often (e.g. every minute for every device) especially if there are many devices, hence the use of symmetric cryptography for this part. As discussed in [4], this is also a way to mitigate the relative weakness of the directory server being a single point of failure.

Because it is difficult to keep control over large communities of devices and because LCDP uses some long terms tickets (see 3.3), one global control mechanism is also added. This is one global symmetric key, chosen by the authentication server and shared with the directory server. It is denoted KoD for "*Key of the Day*", stressing the fact that the authentication server regularly changes it, typically on a daily basis. It is used as a mandatory component in the calculation of tickets. Changing KoD invalidates all the previously calculated tickets. This mechanism provides an authoritative way to globally discard all previous trust relations and to force devices acquiring fresh tickets everyday. Also, it can be useful in case of a mass revocation of devices that should quickly become effective. There is one last advantage of using KoD: we do not want to use the time in LCDP, mainly because some other devices do not have reliable time mechanism. In particular it could be difficult to set up tickets with specific time duration. Instead, KoD provides a way to obsolete all tickets in a single operation.

Because "devil lies in the details" we are very suspicious about the security of the KoD part of the protocol. The verification of it is one important motivation for the collaboration with academic team and for the intensive use of formal tools.

3.3. *Putting it altogether*

The specification of LCDP is provided here in the following formats: one generic execution diagram in figure 2 and one ``Alice & Bob'' trace including the formulas for the computation of tickets. In the trace, we assume that a device D_i already is in a LCDP session. Also, we assume an existing secure channel between AS and DS.

1. AS $\rightarrow$ DS: KoD. This happens regularly, for instance once a day, trough a secure channel.
2. $D_1 \rightarrow$ AS: Id_1. D_1 attempts a SSL connection to AS.

3. $AS \rightarrow D_1$: $K_1, Id_1, t_1 = \{K_1, Id_1, n_1\}_{KoD}$. If AS authenticates D_1, it gives it ticket t_1 for communicating with DS. n_1 is a nonce used for anti-replay. KoD is used to prevent generation of false tickets or the replay of old tickets.

4. $D_1 \rightarrow DS$: Id_1, t_1. D_1 authenticates to DS with its ticket. Decrypting the ticket, DS learns the key K_1.

5. $DS \rightarrow D_1$: $\{Id_i, K_{1,i}, t_{1,i}\} = \{Id_1, Id_i, K_{1,i}, n_{1,i}\}_{Ki}\}_{K1}$. For each D_i willing to communicate, DS gives D_1 a specific ticket.

6. $D_1 \rightarrow D_i$: $Id_1, t_{1,i}$. D_1 presents its ticket to D_i.

7. $D_i \rightarrow D_1$: $\{message\}_{K1,i}$. D_i can now securely send a secret message to D_1.

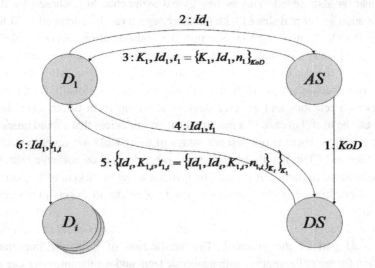

Figure 2: Generic execution diagram of LCDP.

4. Verification of LCDP

4.1. *Formal specification of LCDP*

Before we run manual and automated verifications from AVISPA and SPAN we first need a sufficient specification of LCDP: most of the complexity must be embedded within the specification, otherwise we will miss attacks. On the other hand it shall not become too complex so that tools can handle it correctly and in a reasonable time. As a compromise, we make the following assumptions:

- **SSL is reliable** at least in our context. Thus, at the end of the SSL session between D_i and AS, we can suppose that both parties share one secret key K_{SSLi}.

- **Low number of devices** we set-up LCDP sessions with only a few devices at the same time. Moreover, we restrict the set of devices that will communicate with another to one device at most. This case corresponds to devices that want to communicate by pairs rather than by groups.
- **One directory server** this is an important simplification at the cost of missing attacks that specifically happen with many directory servers.
- **Eluded details** some parts are not formally specified, like the details of the communication between AS and DS, some mechanisms to mitigate consequences of changing KoD, the way devices publish there willingness to communicate with some other.

Remark that these assumptions altogether represent a rather restrictive compromise. Thus it is unlikely that we find an attack, or it will be a very serious one. Our intention is to start with these restrictive assumptions, and then possibly relax some of them, until attacks are eventually found. Doing so, we seek more formal justifications for some protocol features (see end of 4.2).

Taking all above assumptions, we get the HLPSL specification hereafter:

```
Role device1(D1,Di,A,M:agent,Kss11:symmetric_key,Id1:message,
SND,RCV:channel(dy)) played_by D1 def=
    local State:nat,N1,N2,N:text,Idi,Cred,Ticket:message,K1,K1i:symmetric_key
    init State:=0
transition
1.  State=0 /\ RCV(start) =|> State':=1 /\ N':= new() /\SND({Id1.N'}_Kss11)
2.  State=1 /\ RCV({K1'.Id1.N.Cred'}_Kss11) =|> State':=2 /\ SND(Id1.Cred')
3.  State=2 /\ RCV({Idi'.K1i'.Ticket'}_K1) =|> State':= 3 /\ SND(Id1.Ticket')
4.  State=3 /\ RCV({N2'}_K1i) =|> State':= 4
end role


role devicei(Di,D1:agent,Kssli:symmetric_key,Idi:message,SND,RCV:channel(dy))
played_by Di def=
    local State:nat,Msg,N2,N:text,Id1,Cred,Tcred:message,Ki,K1i:symmetric_key
    init State:=0
transition
1.  State=0 /\ RCV(start) =|> State':=1 /\ N':= new() /\SND({Idi.N'}_Kssli)
2.  State=1 /\ RCV({Ki'.Idi.N.Cred'}_Kssli) =|> State':=2 /\ SND(Idi.Cred')
3.  State=2 /\ RCV(Id1'.{Id1'.Idi.K1i'}_Ki) =|> State':=3 /\ Msg':= new() /\
    SND({Msg'}_K1i') /\ secret(Msg',secret_msg,{D1,Di})
end role


role as( A:agent,Kss11,Kssli,KoD:symmetric_key,SND,RCV:channel(dy))
played_by A def=
    local State:nat,N:text,K:symmetric_key,Adr:message
    init State:=0
transition
1.  State=0 /\ RCV({Adr'.N'}_Kssli) =|>
    State':=1 /\ K':= new() /\ SND({K'.Adr'.N'.{K'.Adr'}_KoD}_Kssli)
```

```
2.  State=1 /\ RCV({Adr'.N'}_Kssl1) =|>
    State':=2 /\ K':= new() /\ SND({K'.Adr'.N'.{K'.Adr'}_KoD}_Kssl1)
end role

role ds( M:agent,KoD:symmetric_key,SND,RCV:channel(dy))
played_by M def=
    local State:nat,Idi,Id:message,K,Ki,K1i:symmetric_key
    init State:=0
transition
1.  State=0 /\ RCV(Idi'.{K'.Idi'}_KoD) =|> State':=1
2.  State=1 /\ RCV(Id'.{Ki'.Id'}_KoD) =|> State':=2 /\ K1i':= new() /\
    SND({Id'.K1i'.{Id'.Idi.K1i'}_K}_Ki')
end role

role session(D1,Di,A,M:agent,Kssl1,Kssli,KoD:symmetric_key,Id1,
Idi:message) def=
    local SD1,SDi,SA,SM,RD1,RDi,RC3,RC4,RA,RM:channel(dy)
composition
    device1(D1,Di,A,M,Kssl1,Id1,SD1,RD1) /\ devicei(Di,D1,Kssli,Idi,SDi,RDi)
/\ as(A,Kssl1,Kssli,KoD,SA,RA) /\ ds(M,KoD,SM,RM)
end role

role environment() def=
    const d1,di,i,as,ds:agent,
    oldKssli,newKssl1,newKssli,oldKsslintruder,oldKoD,newKoD:symmetric_key,
    id1,idi,idintruder:message, secret_msg:protocol_id
    intruder_knowledge={i,d1,di,as,ds,id1,idi,idintruder,oldKsslintruder}
composition
    session(i,di,as,ds,oldKsslintruder,oldKssli,oldKoD,idintruder,idi) /\
    session(d1,di,as,ds,newKssl1,newKssli,newKoD,id1,idi)
end role
goal secrecy_of secret_msg end goal
```

4.2. *Verifications using AVISPA and SPAN*

We start the verification of LCDP with a single KoD, hence modeling a "one day" usage. This corresponds to a normal use of LCDP when devices first authenticate, then build trust, and then communicate together. For simulating SSL we first preset symmetric keys between the participating devices and the authentication server. Then, devices systematically use theses keys and a nonce for communicating with AS. The nonce expresses the anti-replay feature of SSL. Hence steps 2 and 3 of LCDP specifications are replaced by:

2. $D_1 \rightarrow AS: \{Id_1, n_1\}_{KSSL1}$.
3. $AS \rightarrow D_1: \{K_1, n_1\}_{KSSL1}, Id_1, t_1 = \{K_1, Id_1, n_1\}_{KoD}$.

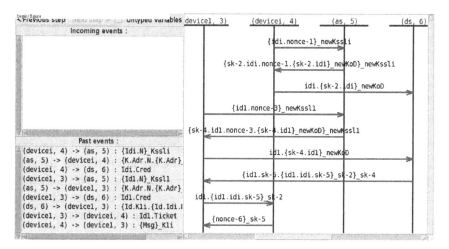

Figure 3: Simple session of LCDP.

The figure 3 shows the corresponding execution with SPAN. We use two of the verification tools from the AVISPA framework: OFMC and ATSE. Note that other tools like SATMC and TA4SP also exist but do not lead to additional result in the context of the present experiment. The verification goal is the secrecy of the messages that are sent between devices. No tool reveals attacks, with respect to the assumptions of 4.1.

We now verify LCDP when a KoD change happens. As indicated in 3.2 we particularly care about potential vulnerabilities in this case. We still use the same method to simulate SSL and we set-up a multiple session using the HLPSL declaration below.

```
session(d1,di,as,ds,oldKssll,oldKssli,oldKoD,idintruder,idi) /\
session(d1,di,as,ds,newKssll,newKssli,newKoD,id1,idi)
```

Note that the same devices **d1** and **di** appear in both sessions. The KoD changes from **oldKoD** in the first session to **newKoD** in the second session. Neither OFMC nor ATSE found attacks in this case.

We also verify the case where one device is valid in the first session, but revoked in the second session. In this case, a device could try to keep its privileges even after revocation and KoD change. We code it by making the intruder **i** explicitly playing the role of a valid device in the first session. In the second session, the intruder is not considered anymore as a valid participant.

However, he is still able to manipulate the network and take advantage of the information gathered during the first session. Here again, no attacks are found. This reads:

```
session(i,di,as,ds,oldKsslintruder,oldKssli,oldKoD,idintruder,idi) /\
session(d1,di,as,ds,newKssl1,newKssli,newKoD,id1,idi)
```

At last, one can argue about the real need of SSL at the beginning of LCDP sessions. Maybe this can be replaced by a lighter mechanism and permanent secret keys. We have tried several ways to downgrade this part. This generally leads to attacks, some of them non trivial. Figure 4 shows such a possible attack, when the anti-replay mechanism at the beginning of LCDP is discarded. We do not give the rational of the attack here, the important fact being the existence of at least one attack when the countermeasure is weakened.

51

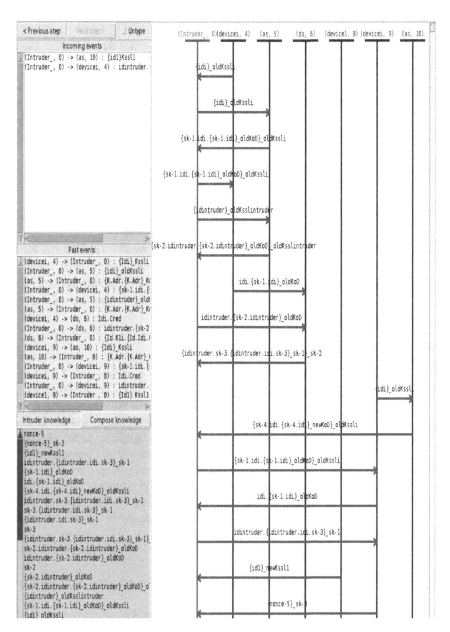

Figure 4: Attack against a slightly downgraded version of LCDP.

5. Conclusion

Both the academic team and the industrial team observe that this experiment has positive results:

- It brings better confidence in the security of LCDP in the simple cases. Neither OFMC nor ATSE found attacks in the test cases. Because ATSE is proven complete [12] this means that, under the simplifying assumptions of section 4.1, there is no attack on a finite number of sessions in the Dolev-Yao model.
- It provides precise justifications for countermeasures that may otherwise be embedded on a rather prophylactic basis. By just removing some countermeasures, we easily get corresponding attacks.
- It produces precise specification and execution diagrams. Both are useful for the understanding and further implementation of LCDP.

Of course, because of many simplifying assumptions, we are still far away from a complete proof of the protocol. The next step is to progressively relax some of the assumptions, especially the one about the number of directory servers. We are also in the course of simulating more devices and larger sets of trusted devices, at the cost of more intensive computation.

References

1. A. Armando, D. Basin, Y. Boichut, Y. Chevalier, L. Compagna, J. Cuellar, P. Hankes Drielsma, P.-C. Héam, O. Kouchnarenko, J. Mantovani, S. Mödersheim, D. von Oheimb, M. Rusinowitch, J. Santos Santiago, M. Turuani, L. Viganò, and L. Vigneron. The AVISPA Tool for the automated validation of internet security protocols and applications, In K. Etessami and S. Rajamani, editors, 17th International Conference on Computer Aided Verification, CAV'2005, volume 3576 of Lecture Notes in Computer Science, pages 281-285, Edinburgh, Scotland, 2005. Springer.
2. Y. Boichut, T. Genet, Y. Glouche, and O. Heen. Using Animation to Improve Formal Specifications of Security Protocols. In Joint conference SAR-SSI, 2007.
3. M. Burrows, M. Abadi, and R. Needham. A logic of authentication. ACM Trans. Comput. Syst., 8(1):18-36, 1990.
4. B. Crispo, B. Popescu, and A. Tanenbaum. Symmetric key authentication services revisited, 2004.
5. D. Dolev and A. Yao. On the security of public key protocols. In Proc. IEEE Transactions on Information Theory, pages 198-208, 1983.
6. W. Diffie and M. Hellman. New directions in cryptography. IEEE Transactions on Information Theory, IT-22(6):644-654, 1976.

7. Y. Glouche and T. Genet. SPAN - a Security Protocol ANimator for AVISPA - User Manual. IRISA / Université de Rennes 1, 2006. 20 pages. http://www.irisa.fr/lande/genet/span/.

8. O. Heen, J.P. Andreaux, and N. Prigent. Improving secure device insertion in home ad-hoc networks. In IFIP SEC, pages 381-394, 2004.

9. G. Lowe. Breaking and Fixing the Needham-Schroeder public-key protocol using FDR. In Tools and Algorithms for the Construction and Analysis of Systems (TACAS), volume 1055, pages 147-166. Springer-Verlag, Berlin Germany, 1996.

10. R. M. Needham and M. D. Schroeder. Using Encryption for Authentication in Large Networks of Computers. Communications of the ACM, 21(12):993-999, 1978.

11. N. Prigent, C. Bidan, J.P. Andreaux, and O. Heen. Secure long term communities in ad hoc networks. In SASN '03: Proceedings of the 1st ACM workshop on Security of ad hoc and sensor networks, pages 115-124, New York, NY, USA, 2003.

12. M. Turuani. Security of Cryptographic Protocols: Decidability and Complexity. PhD thesis, Université of Nancy 1, 2003.

13. M. Weiser. The computer for the 21st century. SIGMOBILE Mob. Comput. Commun. Rev., 3(3):3-11, 1999.

A PERFORMANCE-BASED APPROACH TO SELECTING A SECURE SERVICE DISCOVERY ARCHITECTURE

SLIM TRABELSI

Institut Eurecom, 2229 route des Crêtes, BP 193, 06904 Sophia-Antipolis, France

GUILLAUME URVOY KELLER, YVES ROUDIER

Institut Eurecom, 2229 route des Crêtes, BP 193, 06904 Sophia-Antipolis, France

YVES ROUDIER

Institut Eurecom, 2229 route des Crêtes, BP 193, 06904 Sophia-Antipolis, France

Service discovery, an essential building block of nomadic and ubiquitous computing applications, needs to be secured to be effectively deployed. Centralized and decentralized approaches have been proposed to this end. This paper analyzes the application layer secure matching function using a Markovian performance model in order to analyze various deployment scenarios. This study outlines the determinant parameters that should be evaluated for selecting one out of these two architectures in order to ensure a scalable and efficient service discovery.

1. Introduction

The deployment of ubiquitous computing systems, as notably envisioned by Mark Weiser [1], and the trend towards Service Oriented Architectures will undoubtedly generalize the need for discovery mechanisms as essential components for locating ambient and location-based services. Service discovery in a network can be implemented in two manners, first using a decentralized architecture relying on broadcast or multicast communication, and second using a centralized architecture based on an identified registry relied upon by users and servers to facilitate discovery request matching. The choice of the appropriate architecture to enable an efficient service discovery highly depends on the deployment environment (LAN, wireless or ad-hoc communications, Internet, VPN, etc.) and on parameters like the expected number of users and services, the type and amount of resources available (CPU, memory ...), and the power consumption of user devices. The performance of discovery mechanisms has already been studied through simulation: [2] and [3] present an evaluation of the performance of post-query discovery strategies in ad-hoc networks, while [4] introduces a service discovery performance model that makes it possible to predict discovery service failure and overload in real time. Numerous service discovery standards like WS-Discovery, Jini, UPnP, SLP, or UDDI have also been proposed in recent years, even though their performance has not been assessed analytically to our knowledge. This approach falls short for taking into account the increasing use of discovery in open ubiquitous computing scenarios with numerous new threats [5] [6]. This paper analyzes security mechanisms introduced in [7] and [8] to deal with such issues using performance results obtained out of a Markovian models detailed in [9]. While this model does not take into account low-level network artifacts such as delay or losses, it can assess the impact of introducing security mechanisms at the application level and the resulting processing and traffic overhead incurred. It thus makes it possible to reason about the preferred architecture to ensure an efficient and scalable deployment of secure service discovery depending on specific scenarios.

2. Secure Service Discovery Models

Service discovery involves a service requester (client) and a service provider (server), the latter providing one or multiple services that can be accessed by the clients. In traditional discovery approaches, security is usually limited to recommendations about classical message authentication and integrity protection, thereby implicitly restricting discovery to known services. Ubiquitous computing has prompted standard-independent studies aimed at securing service discovery using an infrastructure for establishing the trustworthiness of clients and services. For instance, Zhu et al. [10] assume that participants to the discovery protocol are located behind a trusted proxy that sets up trust relationships through key exchanges with other proxies. [12] instead suggests the use of a central entity that combines the roles of a Certificate Authority and of a registry, and that helps clients and servers to set up a trust relationship and to establish secure channels with each another. These solutions are not adapted to decentralized architectures and address server rather than client security, contrary to [7] and [8] on which we focus. These security solutions being destined to a wireless environment, they aim at protecting discovery systems against illegal access to discovery messages which the adversary can get. Similarly to these solutions, we consider that brute force DoS and signal jamming are out of scope of our adversarial model. The following sections introduce queuing models of these two approaches.

2.1. *Centralized Discovery Model*

Centralized discovery approaches rely on a registry which plays the role of a trusted third party in charge of enforcing security policies provided by clients and services. Clients and services send their discovery policies to the registry that will be in charge of judging whether a discovery matching is secure.

The queuing model depicted in Figure 1 represents the processing phase of a secure client service request at the registry for a centralized configuration, considering a sole thread is in charge of all processing steps.

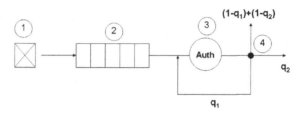

Figure 1: Centralized Model

The discovery process consists of four steps:
1. Client service discovery requests arrival: requests are assumed to be generated according to arrival process with a rate λ.
2. Buffering: The registry can temporarily store the requests to be processed by the central unit. Messages are served in a FIFO manner.
3. Request processing: the registry first matches a client request with the service profiles available locally. The matched service will be authenticated in order to verify its compliance with the security policy provided by the client. If the verification is successful, the registry also has to further authenticate the client in order to verify its compliance with the security policy provided by the service. The corresponding service time is a random variable with a mean value $1/\mu$.
4. Probabilistic decisions (acceptance/rejection): q1 is the probability that a service matches with a client request and be compliant with its policy, q2 the probability that a client be compliant with this service policy.

2.2. *Decentralized Discovery Model*

The security solution proposed in [8] for a decentralized configuration relies on a particular usage of the Attribute Based Encryption mechanism [11]. This mechanism is used by clients to protect their requests by encrypting them according to a particular policy of disclosure of client/service profile attributes.

The queuing model depicted in Figure 2 represents the decentralized discovery scheme in which some computing time is now allocated to encryption and decryption. Requests are routed using multicast, which adds complexity to event handling. In such a decentralized architecture, nodes usually have limited capacities as compared to a registry. For this reason, we considered in our model that a server does not buffer new requests when it is busy. The execution proceeds as follows:

1. Client service discovery request arrival: requests are generated according to an arrival process with rate λ.
2. Servers message processing: all the available servers are contacted by the client via multicast. Each of these servers has to decrypt the messages in order to authenticate and access to client's request. The time to decrypt is assumed to be a random variable with a mean value $1/\mu 1$.
3. Service authentication: q1 is the probability to successfully decrypt a client request. In case of success the server has to encrypt the response message to the client.
4. Client authentication: q2 is the success decryption probability of a client.

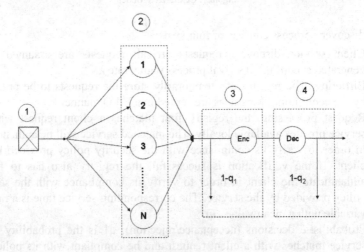

Figure 2: Decentralized Model

3. Matching Probabilities

The probabilities q1 and q2 described above represent the probability for a client or a service to obtain a successful matching (including authentication, access control, decryption) with security policies protecting the access to resource profiles. This probability depends on the number of elements of the systems and on the volume of vocabulary known by each element. The vocabulary volume is the amount of data knowledge related to a certain domain. For example, a subset of the medical vocabulary (scanner, radiology, dermatology, cardiology etc.) can be related to the services deployed inside a hospital building or the roles of users (surgeon, patient, etc.). In analogy to such concepts, we define a vocabulary as the global set of possible identities or roles in a system. The subset of this vocabulary is represented by the group of identities and roles existing in the system.

The probability to match an element (client or au server), represented by a group of attributes x in a system, is defined by the probability P that these attributes belong to the subset vocabulary C part of the general vocabulary V:

$$P(x) = \frac{\binom{x}{C}}{\binom{x}{V}}; size(x) \geq 1 \qquad (1)$$

4. Performance Analysis

Markov chains corresponding to the two queuing models were detailed and validated with a continuous time simulator in [9]. This mathematical model makes it possible to study the performance parameters of service discovery and to determine whether a centralized or a decentralized strategy should be adopted.

The performance study detailed below answers the following determinant questions for selecting one of the two secure solutions to service discovery: in which conditions is the request rejection rate better or worse? Which model is able to serve the largest number of clients? What is the fastest approach? What is the impact of a variable number of servers in the system? What is the impact of the matching probabilities on the performance?

4.1. *System Setup*

This relies on measurements obtained on real systems as previously published. Four test scenarios are described in Table 1. The Attribute Based Encryption/ Decryption duration are excerpted from [11] according to set values for $x=\{1,2,3\}$. We experimented ourselves with XACML policy reasoning and enforcement as detailed in [7]. The arrival rate of client requests, number of services, vocabulary size, and matching probability q1 are variable in our tests.

60

Table1: Values of the input variables used in the tests.

	Centr1	Decentr1	Centra2	Decentr2	Centr3	Decentr3	Centr4	Decentr4
λ	0.5 → 40	0.5 → 40	0.5 → 40	0.5 → 40	0.5 → 40	0.5 → 40	0.5 → 40	0.5 → 40
$\mu 1$	14.28	2.5	14.28	2.5	14.28	2.5	14.28	2.5
$\mu 2$	-	20	-	20	-	20	20	20
V	10	10	10	10	20	20	20	20
C	5	5	8	8	16	16	5	5
$q1$	0.5	0.5	0.8	0.8	0.8	0.8	0.25	0.25
Buffer Size	2-5-10	-	2-5-10	-	2-5-10	-	2-5-10	-

4.2. Rejection Rate

We compare the average rejection rate representing the probability for a client request to be rejected from a server before the processing phase. Rejection occurs when all the servers in the decentralized model are busy, i.e.,

$$R_d = P(N) \qquad (2)$$

and when N slots of the registry cache are occupied in the centralized model,

$$R_c = P(N,0) + P(N,1) \qquad (3)$$

Figure 3 shows that the rejection rate due to a lack of resources is invariant for the centralized model in case of a fixed buffer size; in contrast, as the buffer size increases, the rejection rate reduces. Regarding the decentralized model, Figures 3-a, 3-b, and 3-c show that the rejection rate is strongly dependent on the number of servers deployed. As the number of servers increases, the rejection rate decreases. Figure 3-d shows that probability q1 does not affect the rejection rate for the decentralized model but clearly impacts the rejection rate for the centralized model. We can conclude that the decentralized system is more suitable in a system with a large number of servers.

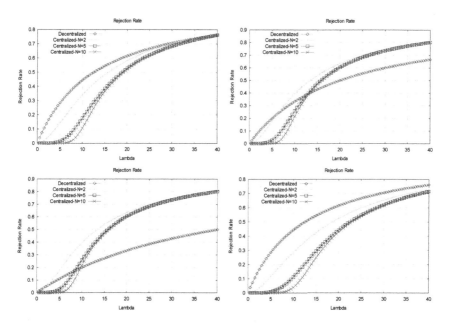

Figure 3: Rejection rate curves for the four test scenarios

4.3. *Average Number of Users in the System*

The average number of users Q present in the system is the temporal mean N(t) of the number of users observed in the system over period [0,T].

$$Q(T) = \frac{1}{T} \sum_n n \cdot T(n, T) \tag{4}$$

In the centralized Markov chain model, Equation (4) can be written as:

$$Q_c = \sum_{n=1}^{Nbuffer} n \cdot \left(p(n, 0) + p(n, 1) \right) \tag{5}$$

In the decentralized Model this equation becomes:

$$Q_d = \sum_{n=1}^{Nservers} n \cdot p(n) \tag{6}$$

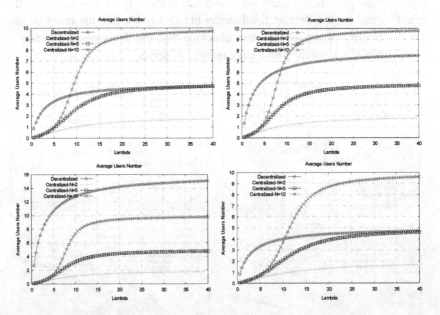

Figure 4: Average number of users in the system for the four test scenarios

Figure 4 illustrates the capacity to serve requests. In the centralized system, it is proportional to the buffer size and to the matching probability (the bigger the matching rate, the longer requests stay in the system). In the decentralized system, the number of users served is proportional to the number of servers and the matching probability does not affect the number of users in the system.

4.4. Service Time Duration of a Request in the System

The lifetime R of a request in the system is the mean time spent by the requests accepted and processed during time period [0,T]. This rate can be computed using Little's Law that states that *"the long-term average number of customers in a stable system Q is equal to the long-term average arrival rate X multiplied by the long-term average time a customer spends in the system R"* [13]:

$$R = \frac{Q}{X} \qquad (6)$$

where X is the product of the probability of at least a user being served and of the Processing Rate. For the centralized model, the service time rate R is:

$$R_c = \frac{Q_c}{\sum\limits_{n=1}^{Nbufer} \left[p(n,0).(1-q1) + p(n,1) \right].\mu} \qquad (7)$$

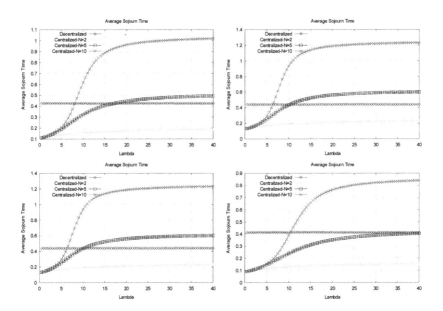

Figure 5: Service time duration of a request in the system for the four tests scenarios

For the decentralized model, the service time rate R is:

$$R_d = \frac{Q_d}{\displaystyle\sum_{n=1}^{Nservers} \mu.p(n)} \tag{8}$$

As depicted in Figure 5, the service time duration is strongly related to the matching probability in the centralized model. As this probability increases, the longer it takes to process the request. With a small buffer size, the system delivers a quicker response although with a high rejection rate. In contrast, the decentralized model exhibits a constant service time in every situation: this is due to the facts that tasks are distributed between servers.

4.5. Summary

Table 2 summarizes the tradeoffs from the performance study presented above: it lists the effects of a change in the infrastructure on the performance parameters that influence the quality of service of the service discovery functionality. One important result of this study is that no single approach can satisfy the requirements of all deployment scenarios.

Table 2: Performance summary (C : Centralized, D: Decentralized, + : increase, - : decrease, = : unchanged value)

Performance parameters:	Reject		Number of users		Service Time	
	C	D	C	D	C	D
Increased Buffer Size	-	=	+	=	+	=
Increased Matching Probability	=	=	-	=	+	=
Increased Number of Servers	=	-	=	+	=	=

5. Conclusion

This paper evaluated the performance of the secure service discovery function, a basic building block in nomadic and ubiquitous computing, as deployed with two approaches: a centralized one, requiring the setup of a trusted third party, the registry; a decentralized one, relying only on a decentralized matching by services themselves. To our knowledge, this is the very first evaluation of the performance of service discovery that takes into account the cost of secure matching and that compares these two different techniques using a Markovian model. This study provides determinant elements for selecting and fine-tuning either of these approaches in order to ensure the scalability of service discovery according to the application scenario deployment parameters. We plan to evaluate the impact of blind DoS attacks on the system by considering a malicious traffic class representing fake encrypted messages.

References

1. Weiser, M.: The Computer of the 21st Century. Scientific American, vol. 265, no. 3, pp. 66-75 (1991)
2. Luo, H., L., Barbeau, M.: Performance Evaluation of Service Discovery Strategies in Ad Hoc Networks. Second Annual Conference on Communication Networks and Services Research pp. 61-68 (2004)
3. Barbeau, M., Kranakis, E.: Modeling and Performance Analysis of Service Discovery Strategies in Ad Hoc Networks. International Conference on Wireless Networks pp. 44-50 (2003)
4. Dabrowski, C., Mills, K.L., Rukhin, A.L.: Performance of Service-Discovery Architectures in Response to Node Failures. Software Engineering Research and Practice, pp. 95-104 (2003)
5. Trabelsi, S., Roudier, Y., Pazzaglia, J.C.: Discovery: Threats and solutions. 2nd Conference on Security in Network Architectures and Information Systems, Annecy, France (2007)
6. Trabelsi, S., Roudier, Y., Pazzaglia, J.C.: Service discovery: Reviewing Threats and Security Architectures. Research Report RR-07/197 (2007)
7. Trabelsi, S., Gomez, L., Roudier, Y.: Context-Aware Security Policy for the Service Discovery. Symposium on Security in Networks and Distributed Systems (SSNDS) Niagara Falls, Canada (2007)
8. Trabelsi, S., Pazzaglia, J.C, Roudier, Y.: Secure Web service discovery: overcoming challenges of ubiquitous computing. 4th IEEE European Conference on Web Services, Zurich - Switzerland (2006)
9. Trabelsi, S., Urvoy-Keller, G., Roudier, Y.: A Markovian performance model for secure service discovery systems. Rapport de recherche RR-08-214. (2008)
10. Zhu, F., Mutka, M., and Ni, L.: Splendor: A secure, private, and locationaware service discovery protocol supporting mobile services. First IEEE International Conference on Pervasive Computing and Communications, pp. 235–242 (2003)
11. Hengartner, U. and Steenkiste, P.: Exploiting Hierarchical Identity-Based Encryption for Access Control to Pervasive Computing Information. Proc. of First IEEE/CreateNet International Conference on Security and Privacy for Emerging Areas in Communication Networks, Athens, Greece, pp. 384-393 (2005)

12. Czerwinski, S.E., et al: An Architecture for a Secure Service Discovery Service. MobiCom, Seattle, WA (1999)
13. Little, J. D. C.: A Proof of the Queueing Formula L = λ W" Operations Research, 9, pp. 383-387 (1961)

A SOLUTION FOR DEFENDING AGAINST DENIAL OF SERVICE ATTACK ON WIRELESS LAN

DINH-THUC NGUYEN

University of Natural Science, Vietnam National
227 Nguyen Van Cu Street, District 5, HCM City, Vietnam

NGOC-BAO TRAN

Faculty of Mathematics and Informatics, HCM City University of Pedagogy 280 An Duong Vuong Street, District 5, HCM City, Vietnam

MINH-DUC NGUYEN-HO

Faculty of Information Technology, Ton Duc Thang University
98 Ngo Tat To Street, Binh Thanh District, HCM City, Vietnam

Wireless local area networks (WLAN) have come into more popular, the security over wireless network is becoming a significant issue. Together with its higher and higher popularity, the internet has also shown more and more weakness of wireless protocols that leads to attacks from "professional" or "amateur" hackers. There are many improving efforts the security of wireless network (from IEEE 802.11 standard protocol to 802.11i building on top of the IEEE 802.1X standard). However, these cannot defend WLAN from denial of service (DoS) attacks. In this paper, we focus on analyzing denial of service attacks on 802.11-based protocols, especially de-authentication and disassociation attacks that called "dis'ing" attacks. There are some of approaches proposed to prevent kind of these attacks by authenticating management frames. Based on simple, efficient and lower cost of deployment on currently 802.11 protocol, we propose a solution for defending against "dis'sing" attack using letter-envelop protocol to authenticate management frames.

1. Introduction

Nowadays, at many places such as buildings, schools, cafes, airport lounges… we easily see the symbol "Wi-Fi" – indicating that wireless network is available. After wireless station (client) has selected an access point to use for communication, it must first authenticate itself to the AP. In the 802.11 protocol, a part of the authentication framework is a message that allows clients and access point to request de-authentication or disassociation from one another.

Unfortunately, this message itself is not authenticated using any keying material, so an attacker may elect to deny access to individual clients, or even rate limit their access, in addition to simply denying service to the entire channel.

DoS attack is a serious threat against availability of network services, and it is difficult to counter. There are two main reasons that 802.11-based wireless systems are vulnerable to DoS attacks [2], [3], [6]: lack of physical boundaries for radio waves or lack of frame authentication in 802.11 management frames, which are called "dis'ing" attacks. The first reason makes wireless networks are susceptible to RF jamming. The normal ranges for 802.11-based communications are 2.4 GHz (for 802.11b and g) or 5GHz (for 802.11a). A high-powered rouge signal can interferes with the network's existing radio transmissions. This is out of scope of our goals. Let us focus on the second reason. According to [4], [5], [7] there are four proposal approaches for preventing the "dis'ing" attack:

- Disable de-authentication and disassociation frame function. This approach required updating the firmware of devices to ignore de-authentication and disassociation frame send (receive) to (from) Access Point. Up to now, we have not seen any applications for WLAN using this approach.
- De-authentication and disassociation frame queue
- Upgrade authentication server for processing disassociation frame. In this approach, we must install a central manager (CM) to manage and control Access point and wireless stations. CM is a backend server that played as an authentication server in 802.1X model. These approaches required higher deployment cost. On the other hand, we must build a secure channel for communicating between Access Point and Central Manager. They also have weakness called *single server failure*.
- Authenticate de-authentication and disassociation frame. There are some of researches have been proposed on 802.1X protocol, these approaches just focus on authenticating EAP (Extensible Authentication Protocol) management frame. In [6] Shiguo Wan et al. proposed a solution for authenticating by replacing from Application level to Data Link level of TCP/IP 802.11 protocol. These solutions can solve some of DoS problems. However, they have not solved capability of the system yet, because they still have memory and computation DoS attacks.

In this paper, we propose a solution for defending against "dis'sing" attack using protocol, called letter-envelop protocol, to authenticate management frames. The proposed solution and letter-envelop protocol will be detailed in following sections.

2. Letter-envelope protocol

Alice and Bob are playing chess over the internet. They want to interrupt the game for the night. Alice has to send Bob some messages to encode her last move, say $m = m_1 m_2 \ldots m_t$. The next morning, she has to give some key, which allows Bob to reconstruct her move. Bob should not be able to reconstruct Alice's move without the key; Alice should not be able to change her last move and modify it.

Alice does as the following:

Alice extends m to a prime number:

$p = m_0 m_1 \ldots m_l m_{l+1} \ldots m_t , \quad (t \gg 1)$

1. Alice also generates another prime q with $t + 2$ digits.
2. Alice computes the product $N = pq$.
3. Alice sends N to Bob.
4. To continue the play, Alice has to send q to Bob.
5. Bob checks if $q | N$ then Bob calculates $p = N / q$ and picks m from p.

This protocol works because:

- The first, Alice cannot change her last move. This is because N contains all the information about her move. So Alice commits herself to the move when sending N.
- Bob cannot see to have the advantage because he has to find prime factors of a large number N.
- Can Alice cheat by sending a different pair (p', q') of primes the next time? No, because Bob can easily compute the product of $p'q'$, and check that this is indeed the number N that was sent the previous time.

By the letter-envelope scheme, to reconstruct m one has to find out p from the given N , this factorization problem is the intractable problem if p and q be large prime numbers. But when we know p and/or q , we could find out q , so we can read m because the division is a trivial task for a computer. For using this scheme one needs large prime numbers. We know that there is not the largest primes [8], but are there any with t-digits, starting with l-digits of given m? We have a positive answer by the follow proposition.

<u>Proposition</u> Among t-digits numbers, one in about every $2.3t$ is a prime.

To prove this proposition, we use the prime number theorem that proved by Hadamand and Vallee-Poussin in 1896.

<u>Theorem</u> (The Prime Number Theorem)

Let $\pi(n)$ denote the number of prime among 1, 2… n, then $\pi(n) \cong \dfrac{n}{\ln n}$

Proof of proposition: Now we can prove proposition

Let $\gamma(t)$ denote the number of prime with t-digits. By the above Prime Number Theorem, we have:

$$\gamma(t) = \frac{10^t}{t\ln 10} - \frac{10^{t-1}}{(t-1)\ln 10} = \frac{(9t-10)10^{t-1}}{t(t-1)\ln 10}$$

Since

$$\frac{9t-10}{t-1} = 9 - \frac{1}{t-1}$$

is very close to 9 if t is large, we get that the number of primes with t-digits is approximately

$$\gamma(t) = \frac{9t-10}{(t-1)} \frac{10^{t-1}}{t\ln 10} \approx 9\frac{10^{t-1}}{t\ln 10}$$

Comparing this with the total number of positive integers with t-digits, which we know is $10^t - 10^{t-1} = 9 \times 10^{t-1}$, we get

$$\frac{9 \times 10^{t-1}}{t \times \ln 10 \times 9 \times 10^{t-1}} = \frac{1}{\ln 10 \times t} \approx \frac{1}{2.3t}$$

It follows that $\gamma(t) \approx 2.3t$

We use the following theorem to construct generating prime algorithm.

Theorem

Let

$$n-1 = F \times R = \left(\prod_{i=1}^{s} p_i^{a_i}\right) R,$$

where $R < \sqrt{n}$

Suppose further that it exist b so that:

 (i) $b^{n-1} \equiv 1 \ (mod \ n)$

 (ii) $\gcd\left(b^{(n-1)/p_i} - 1, n\right) = 1, \ t = 1,2,...,s$

Then n is a prime number

Proof

• Let p be the least prime so that $n = pN$, and let d be the least integer:
• $b^d \equiv 1 \ [mod \ p]$, we have $d|(p-1)$
• By (i), $d|(n-1)$
• But by (ii) $d:(n-1)/p$
• $d|(p-1) \Rightarrow F|(p-1) \Rightarrow p-1 \geq F \geq \sqrt{n} \Leftrightarrow p = n$

Algorithm

• Input: $t \in N^+, m = m_0 m_1 ... m_i \in N, (t \gg l)$
• Output: p is a prime with t-digits.

Starting with $m_0 m_1 \ldots m_i$

1. Generates q with $\frac{t}{2}+1$ digit, starting with $m_0 m_1 \ldots m_t$
2. Choose $r < q : 1 + rq \equiv \pm 1 (mod\ 6)$; and let $p = rq + 1$
3. If pseudo-prime (p)
   Then by the above Theorem $(p-1) = \pi \times R$,
   Return p
4. $r = r + 6$
5. go to (3)

<u>Subroutine</u> pseudo-prime (n)

- Input:
  $$n = 2m + 1, m \in N^+$$
  $$P = \{2,3,5,\ldots\} : \text{set of } k\text{-first primes}$$
- Output
  n is a prime number?
  1. Select randomly b from P
  2. Choose m be odd integer: $n - 1 = 2^r m$
  3. For $i = 1 \to r$ do
     If $(b^{2^i m} \bmod n \neq \pm 1)$ Return false
  4. Return true

This subroutine used Fermat's theorem to check whether n $(n \in N^+)$ is a pseudo-prime.

3. Proposed Solution

Our solution is an addition on current 802.11-based protocol. To prevent the disassociation attack, we use letter-envelop protocol to authenticate management frames in association process. After authentication process between wireless station and access point, our association process takes place.

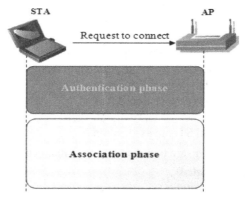

Figure 1. WLAN access control

Throughout this paper, we will use the following notations:

- STA is wireless station, who wants to join the wireless network;
- AP is access point;
- p, q are strong random prime numbers generated by STA when it wants to associate with AP and $N = pq$;
- p_i, q_i are strong random prime numbers generated by AP when STA wants to associate with AP and $N_i = p_i q_i$;
- p_s, q_s are strong random prime numbers generated by AP when it boot or restart and $N_s = p_s q_s$;
- $b|a$ is $a \equiv 0 \pmod{b}$.

3.1. *Association*

As the mentioned above, after authenticating phase between wireless station and access point, our association process takes place using letter-envelop protocol to authenticate association frame. Figure 2 shows the process of association.

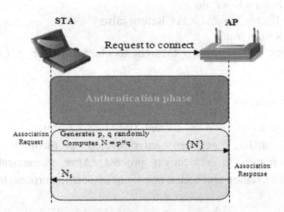

Figure 2. Association process

1. STA generates two random prime numbers p, q, then computes $N(N = pq)$, and sends N to AP in association request message.
2. AP check STA's ID
   a) If exists in AID (Association ID) table
      1. Stores N in STA's entry in AID table;
      2. Sends N_s to STA in association response message ($N_s = p_s q_s$ where p_s, q_s are two random prime numbers generated by AP when it started).
   b) Otherwise, it aborts.
3. STA checks and stores N_s

3.2. *Disassociation*

In current 802.11-based protocol, the disassociation and de-authentication packets have the same structures just differ from the reason codes as in table 3.1.

Table 1. Reason code

Code	Meaning
0	Reserved
1	Unspecified reason
2	Previous authentication no longer valid
3	De-authenticated because sending station is leaving (or has left) IBSS or ESS
4	Disassociated due to inactivity
5	Disassociated because AP is unable to handle all currently associated stations
6	Class 2 frame received from non-associated station
7	Class 3 frame received from non-associated station
8	Disassociated because sending station is leaving (or has left) BSS
9	Station requesting (re)association is not authenticated with responding station
10-65535	Reserved

There are three situations to disassociate from the network:
- The STA wants to leave off network, in this case the reason code is 3 or 8;
- The AP goes offline, in this case the reason code is 3;
- These others:
  - Reason code is 2, 6, 7 or 9: in this case the STA have not authenticated or associated with the AP yet, so the STA will be ignored the disassociation packet from the AP.
  - Reason code is unspecified: AP and STA will be ignored disassociation and de-authentication packets;
  - Reason code is 5: AP sends disassociation packet to some of currently connected STAs when it cannot handle all associated STAs.

Case 1 (Reason code = 3 or 8): Once the STA wants to leave off network, the disassociation procedure will execute as the following:
1. STA sends disassociation frame including the value p to AP.
2. AP find out STA's N in ID table, then checks whether $p|N$
   a) If $p|N$ then remove STA's entry and STA is disassociated
   b) Otherwise, it aborts

With this solution, if an attacker wants to spoof STA's MAC address and send disassociation to AP, he must have the correct value p, assuming that he eavesdrops and gets N, he cannot find the prime factors of a large number N

(proof in section 2). That means attacker cannot get the correct value p and he cannot spoof legitimate STA to send disassociation frame.

Case 2 (Reason code = 3): Once the AP goes offline it broadcast disassociated frame (reason code=3) including the value p_s to all STA. Based on reason code, each STA check whether $p_s|N_s$. If $p_s|N_s$, STA disconnect to AP; otherwise, the STA aborts.

Similar to spoofing STA' MAC in case 1, if an attacker wants to spoof AP's MAC address and send disassociation frame to STA, he must have the correct value p_i or p_s. He eavesdrops and gets N_i or N_s; he cannot also find the prime factors of a large number N_i, N_s (proof in section 2). That means attacker cannot get the correct value p_i or p_s and he cannot spoof legitimate AP to send disassociation frame.

Case 3 (Reason code = 5): AP sends disassociation packet to some of currently connected STAs when it cannot handle all associated STAs (case 3).

- With the system used pre-shared key authentication mode we extended association process as in figure 3:

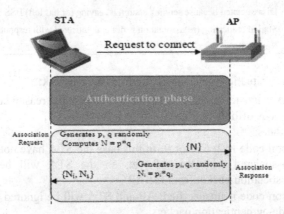

Figure 3. Association process in pre-shared key mode

Once the AP wants to disassociate with an individual STA, the disassociation procedure will also execute as the following:

1. *AP sends disassociation frame including the value p_i to STA.*
2. *Based on the reason code in this frame, STA checks whether $p_i|N_i$*
   a) If $p_i|N_i$ then STA do disassociates with AP
   b) Otherwise, it aborts

Note that STA will discard any disassociation frame when its status is not associated.

- With the system used 802.1X authentication mode, we do not use extended solution as in figure 3. Because the extended solution has computation DoS on AP when attacker sends association request continuously. Therefore, we keep the original proposed as in figure 2 and will ignore disassociation packet in this situation. Because we think that this case is rarely occur and hardly to deploy the 802.1X authentication mode in public places.

4. Implementation and Evaluation

We implemented in C and tested the proposed solution in Linux environment. In implementation, we just modify the format of the original 802.11 management frames by appending the authenticating value N or N_s after the current data in association request or association response of frame body section of management frame. Figure 4 is illustrated the structures of management frame in original 802.11 protocol and our proposal. We developed two modules as the following:

- *Access Point Module* installed in the PC with Wireless network card included. The module plays a role as an Access Point to authorize access right for the wireless devices. As mentioned previous section, we integrated our solution with open and pre-shared key authentication mode.
- *Station Module* installed in the wireless station that communicated with the AP Module when it connects to the network.

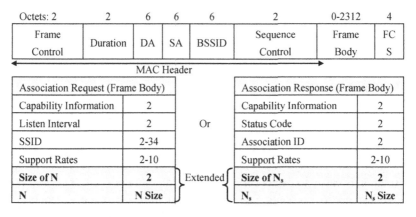

Figure 4. Format of our proposal 802.11 management frame [9]

Nowadays, there are many tools on the internet that can use to launch flooding and "dis'ing" attacks such as WLAN-jack, Void11, FATA-jack, AirJack, File2air, CommView for WiFi...

For the testing, we use *CommView for WiFi* tool to do flooding and "dis'ing" attacks on original 802.11 protocol (without authenticate management frame) and on the proposed solution.

- Case 1: Attacking on the original 802.11 protocol, here are results
  - Flooding attack type (AP overload): the AP stops temporal in 2-3 seconds
  - Dis'ing attack type: the STA will be disconnected to the network.
- Case 2: Attacking on our proposed solution

The system architecture for attacking on proposed solution as below
  - One PC (CPU Intel Celeron 3.0GHz, RAM 1GB, HDD 80GB) which installed *Access Point Module* plays as an Access Point
  - One PC (CPU Intel Celeron 1.73 GHz, RAM 512 GB, HDD 80GB) which installed *Station Module* active as a wireless station
  - One PC (CPU Intel Core Duo 1.6 GHz, RAM 512 GB, HDD 80GB) run CommView for Wifi to attack to systems

Similar to attacking on the original 802.11 protocol, we do the same flooding and dis'ing attacks on proposed implementation system. The system can prevent these attack types. Table 2 describes experimental results.

Table 2. Experimental results

Size of N (bits)	Defending against Dis'ing attack	
	AP	Wireless client
128	Yes	Yes
256	Yes	Yes
512	Yes	Yes
1024	Yes	Yes

5. Conclusion

We have presented a solution for Defending against DoS Attack on Wireless LAN. The proposed solution is an addition on current 802.11-based protocol. To prevent the disassociation attack, we use letter-envelop protocol to authenticate management frames in association process. Furthermore, our solution is easily to deploy. It is only an addition in now 802.11-based protocol. We just modify association request/response message to gain defending WLAN against DoS attack. This requires wireless systems update their firmware.

References

1. Andrew A.Vladimirov, Konstantin V.Gavrilenko, Andrei A.Mikhailopsky, "The secrets of Wireless Hacking", *Adddison-Wesley*, 2004.

2. Kevin Beaver and Peter T.Davis, "Hacking wireless networks for Dummies", *Wiley Publishing*, 2005.
3. John Bellardo and Stefan Savage, "802.11 Denial-of-Service Attacks: Real Vulnerabilities and Practical Solutions", *Proceedings of the 12th USENIX Security Symposium*, Washington, D.C., USA August 4–8, 2003.
4. Ping Ding, JoAnne Holliday, Aslihan Celik, "Improving the Security of Wireless LANs by Managing 802.1x Disassociation", *Proceedings of the IEEE Consumer Communications and Networking Conference*, Las Vegas, NV, January 2004.
5. Chibiao Liu, James T. Yu, "An Analysis of DoS Attacks on Wireless LAN", *Proceedings of the IASTED International Multi-Conference on Wireless and Optical Communications*, Banff, Alberta, Canada, 2006.
6. Zhiguo Wan, Bo Zhu, Robert H.Deng, Feng Bao, Akkihebbal Ananda, "DoS-Resistant Access Control Protocol with Identity Confidentiality for Wireless Network", *Proceeding of the IEEE Wireless Communications and Networking Conference,* New Orleans, LA, USA, 13-17 March 2005.
7. Ge, Wenfeng, S. Sampalli, "A Novel Scheme for Prevention of Management Frame Attacks on Wireless LANs", *Master Thesis, Dalhousie University*, March 29, 2005.
8. S.Y.Yan, "Number theory for computing", *Springer*, 2000.
9. LAN MAN Standards Committee of the IEEE Computer Society, "Part 11: Wireless LAN Medium Access Control (MAC) and Physical Layer (PHY) Specifications", 2003.